G000162565

The Little Book of

Design
Classics

This edition published by Carlton Books Limited 2002
20 Mortimer Street
London W1T 3JW

A catalogue record for this book is available from
the British Library.

ISBN 1 84222 537 5

Printed in Singapore

The Little Book of

Design

Classics

Catherine McDermott

CARLTON

Contents

6	Swiss Army Knife
7	Rug Design – Archibald Knox
8	Colman's Mustard Packaging
9	Casa Battló Apartments
10	Glasgow School of Art
11	AEG Poster
12	Coca Cola Bottle
13	London Underground Type
14	Red and Blue Armchair
15	Merz Magazine
16	Quaker Oats Packaging
17	Burberry
18	Chanel No.5 Perfume Bottle
19	Bauhaus School Building
20	Cesca Chair
21	E1027 Side Table
22	Cornish Ktchenware
23	Nord Express Poster
24	Chaise Longue
25	Barcelona Chair
26	Chrysler Building
27	Electric Light Bulbs Fabric
28	Campbell's Soup Can
29	Lieca Camera
30	Anglepoise Lamp
31	Glass Teapot
32	Pressed Glass 4644
33	Marion Dorn Rug
34	Poster for London Underground
35	Poster for Shell
36	Stacking Stool "L" Leg
37	Dutch Post Office Graphics
38	Ekco Ad 65 Radio
39	Falling Water
40	American Modern Table Service
41	Hudson J-3a Train
42	Bruton Electric Fire
43	Lucky Strike Cigarette Pack
44	Vespa
45	Witchita House
46	Dior – The New Look
47	La Pavoni Coffee Machine
48	Eames House
49	Arabesque Table
50	Penguin Book Covers
51	Ericofon
52	Eames Storage Unit 421 C
53	Tupperware
54	Milk Bottle
55	Skylon
56	No 22 Diamond Chair
57	P40 Reclining Armchair
58	Model H Lamp
59	Routemaster Bus

60	Notre Dame de Haut
61	Ant Chair
62	Luminator Lamp
63	Seagram Building
64	K2 Kettle
65	Anatomy of a Murder Poster
66	Mini
67	TWA Terminal Building
68	Action Office
69	Mini-Skirt
70	Air France Poster
71	Mother and Child Graphics
72	Cylinda Line Tea Service
73	Family Dog Poster
74	Concorde
75	Galvez House
76	Brionvega Black ST/201
77	3089 A.B.C. Graduating Table Bowls
78	Totem Stereo
79	Tizio Table Lamp
80	Beogram 4000 Turntable
81	Sydney Opera House
82	Pompidou Centre
83	Sony Walkman
84	Table with Wheels
85	Carlton Sideboard
86	Dyson Dual Cyclone
87	Swatch
88	Ya Ya Ho Lighting System
89	Hong Kong and Shanghai Banking Corporation
90	Pasta Set 9092
91	Whistling Kettle 9093
92	Japanese Fashion Design
93	Kidosaki House
94	The Face Magazine
95	S Chair
96	Vitra Design Museum
97	Ty Nant Water Bottle
98	WW Stool
99	Ray Gun Magazine
100	Odeon Cutlery
101	Powerplay Armchair
102	Well Tempered Chair
103	Sardine Collectors' Cabinet
104	Wine Rack
105	Hannibal Tape Dispenser
106	Vivienne Westwood
107	Canon Ixus
108	Apple Imac
109	Treforchette Table Lamp
110	Garbo Waste Bin
111	Eden
112	Acknowledgements

DATE: 1891

DESIGNERS: Carl and Victoria Elsener

MANUFACTURER: The Elsener Family, Switzerland

Swiss Army Knife

With its characteristic bright red body bearing the hallmark white cross, the Swiss Army knife is more than a simple pen-knife: it is a miniature toolbox that folds away and fits into the palm of your hand. Carl and Victoria Elsener manufactured high-quality cutlery at their small factory in the Swiss Alps. In 1891 they were offered a contract by Switzerland's army to provide a sturdy knife for soldiers. The following year they won a second contract. This time they developed the elegant, multi-purpose "Officer's Knife" – the first version of the Swiss Army knife that would sell millions. Four generations of the family have now produced the legendary knives, based on the three original principles – high quality, versatility and design excellence. The basic model is little more than a variety of foldaway blades, while models like the "SwissChamp" include a corkscrew, can and bottle openers, screwdrivers, nail file, wood saw, pliers, scissors, toothpick and chisel.

Rug by Archibald Knox

DATE: 1900
DESIGNER: Archibald Knox (1864–1933)

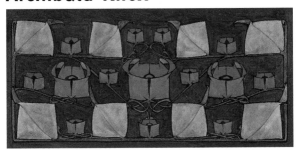

Archibald Knox is probably best known for his turn-of-the-century metalware designs for Liberty's, the famous London department store. His talent as an architect and designer was, however, far more widespread and he is recognized as one of the great exponents of the British Arts and Crafts movement.

In common with his contemporaries, Knox explored the Celtic traditions of his native Isle of Man. This can be seen in his use of complex flowing patterns. However, his style was much more than simple revivalism and, although inspired by the glowing colours and the flowing, sinuous forms of Celtic decoration, Knox went on to create a language of ornament that saw an increasing simplification and refinement of forms.

Designed in 1900, Knox's watercolour sketch for the rug shown here still appears fresh and timeless. Such work positioned Knox not only as a leading Arts and Crafts designer but also as a practitioner who helped to establish a new direction in design for the next century.

Colman's Mustard Packaging

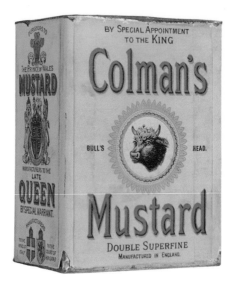

There is some packaging that has become so closely identified with a product that it has come to represent the food itself. Colman's Mustard is one such example. The Norwich firm of J. and J. Colman was founded in 1823. The use of mustard yellow, coupled with the bull's head trademark on the mustard's packaging, ensured that the brand became an immediate success.

Colman's understood a fundamental principle of pack design – the vital role that colour always plays in customer identification of the product. Using the vivid yellow meant that Colman's customers recognized the product before they even registered the bull's head design. The consistent use of the latter has meant that Colman's has maintained its place in the market over the years.

Casa Battló Apartments

DATE: 1905–07
Barcelona, Spain
ARCHITECT: Antoni
Gaudí (1852–1926)

Antoni Gaudí worked almost exclusively in and around his native city of Barcelona. He merged his native Catalan style with Moorish features and natural forms to produce some of the most novel architecture of the late nineteenth and early twentieth century.

His most original version of Catalan Art Nouveau, known as "*Modernismo*", can be seen in the remodelling of an apartment building into a residence for the Battló family, with offices on the ground floor and apartments for rent. Here Gaudí's distinctive language of ornament is no longer simply applied to a building but constitutes the essential structural elements. The façade is covered with highly coloured mosaics, constructed with broken glass, while the roof outline resembles the form of an exotic reptile. Gaudí's highly original use of sculptural form established him as one of the great artist-architects of the twentieth century. However, it should be said that this does not mark the start of something new, rather the culmination of the previous century's obsession with revivalism and natural forms. Nonetheless, Gaudí became an inspirational figure for many Postmodernist architects in the period following the Second World War.

DATE: 1897–1909
Glasgow, Scotland
ARCHITECT: Charles
Rennie Mackintosh
(1868–1928)

Glasgow School of Art

Although Mackintosh is now one of the world's most famous architects, he died in 1928 a neglected figure. It was not until the 1960s that his work was reassessed, and his importance as a key transitional figure from the historicism of the nineteenth century to the abstraction of the early twentieth century acknowledged.

Mackintosh worked closely with his wife, Margaret Macdonald, with whom he trained at the Glasgow School of Art. Their original style very quickly attracted interest from all over the world, particularly the Vienna Secessionists.

Mackintosh's most famous building was the Glasgow School of Art. The first phase, including the entrance shown here, was completed between 1898 and 1899. Huge windows dominate the entrance and the front can be read as an abstracted form of traditional Scottish castle architecture. His distinctive detailing can be seen in the railings and window brackets. The second phase of building was completed in 1909.

AEG
Poster

DATE: 1910
DESIGNER: Peter Behrens (1868–1941)

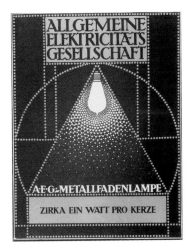

Peter Behrens is important in the history of advertising because he was one of the first poster designers to produce a visual language that articulated new spirit of the twentieth century. When in 1907 he was invited by Emil Rathennau, director of the Allgemeine Elektricitäts-Gesellschaft (AEG), to become its artistic director, he developed the first concept of company corporate identity. From 1907 until 1914 Behrens was responsible for all aspects of the company's output, from architecture to posters and products.

The influence of Behrens was manifold. In 1907 he was a founder member of the Deutsche Werkbund, he designed typefaces and was responsible for one of Germany's earliest Modernist buildings, AEG's steel, glass and concrete turbine factory of 1909. In his position as artistic director he employed some of Europe's brightest young talents, including Le Corbusier, Mies van der Rohe and Walter Gropius.

Coca-Cola Bottle

Many manufacturers believe that shape is the greatest competitive edge a product can have. It identifies products on the shelf and makes them easy to advertise. Perhaps the most famous bottle shape of all time Coca-Cola's.

In 1886, Dr John Pemberton, a pharmacist in Atlanta, Georgia, invented the Coca-Cola formula and a year later Willis Venables, an Atlanta drugstore barman, first mixed Coca-Cola syrup with carbonated water at five cents a glass. Three years later all rights to the product had been bought by Asa Chandler, owner of a pharmaceutical company. Coca-Cola was first bottled in 1894, and legend has it that Pemberton asked his book-keeper to create the handwritten trademark.

The Coca-Cola bottle evolved from 1915, when a Swedish engineer, Alex Samuelson of the Root Glass Company of Terre Haute, Indiana, based the curved shape on an illustration of a cocoa bean found in the *Encyclopedia Britannica*. In 1920 the final version of this design was patented and put into production.

Underground Type

DATE: 1916
DESIGNER: Edward
Johnston (1872–1944)

Edward Johnston is responsible for one of the most famous corporate identity programmes in the world, that belonging to London's Underground system. Based on a font he had designed in 1916 for Frank Pick, London Transport's design manager, it was also Britain's first Modernist typeface using clean, geometric forms that proved easy to read and immensely popular with the public. Arguably it was the first sans serif face of the twentieth century and was deeply influential on British graphic design in general and in particular on Johnston's pupil, the famous sculptor and typeface designer Eric Gill (1882–1940). London's Underground system expanded rapidly after World War One and provided the British public with their first, sometimes only, opportunity to see modern architecture and design. In the 1980s the type was redrawn by Banks and Miles to meet the more complex applications of the 1990s.

DATE: 1918
DESIGNER: Gerrit
Rietveld (1888–1964)
MATERIAL: painted wood

Red and Blue Armchair

Gerrit Rietveld was a member of *De Stijl*
(the Style), one of the most coherent groups
within the Modern Movement. Their search for a
universal form of expression led them to experiment
with primary colours, basic geometric shapes and
abstracted pure forms. The most recognizable
expression of these aims can be found in the
paintings of Piet Mondrian. Rietveld took literally
the *De Stijl* message that "the new consciousness
is ready to be realized in everything, including the
everyday things of life". He developed the ideas
of *De Stijl* in a three-dimensional form, the
most famous expressions of which were the
celebrated Red and Blue chair of 1918, and
the Schröder House built six years later with
Truss Schröder-Schräder in Utrecht. It is simplistic
but nonetheless true to describe these designs
as three-dimensional Mondrian paintings.

Merz
Magazine

DATE: 1920
DESIGNER:
Kurt Schwitters
(1887–1948)

In about 1910 the new ideas emerging from art
and architecture began to have an inevitable effect
on type and design. Just as architecture challenged
the idea that buildings should refer to historical
sources, type designers also experimented with
new forms. Important here were the Italian
Futurists who saw new type design as a way
to "redouble the force of expressive words. Kurt
Schwitters was a leading force behind another art
movement – Dada. Using type he put together a
series of famous collages employing the principle
of random choice. In doing so Schwitters placed
type within a fine art context and opened up the
possibility that type was not only concerned with
function and legibility.

41

Quaker Oats Packaging

The Quaker Mill Company of Ohio, USA, first produced their now-famous Quaker Oats, complete with the instantly recognizable Quaker emblem, in 1877. For Americans the now familiar image of the patriarchal Quaker carried an important message. In a country that prided itself as the refuge for non-conformist religious groups, the Quakers were seen to uphold the values of honesty and fair trading. With this powerful brand image it is not surprising that when in 1890 Quaker Oats was sold to the American Cereal Company, it became their biggest-selling brand, leading in 1900 to a name change: the Quaker Oats Company.

One of the interesting marketing innovations the company introduced was the tradition of free gifts with cereal packs. During the early years of the century the company attracted prospective customers with offers that included free cereal bowls for the required number of pack coupons and this strategy proved such a success that it inspired many trade copycats.

16

Burberry

BURBERRY BOOK, patterns and prices, post free on mention of the "Queen."

The British Burberry is now synonymous with the waterproof mackintosh. Styled like an army overcoat, it became one of the most familiar fashion accessories of the twentieth century, and the brand shows every sign of continuing its huge success in the twenty-first. Its origins go back to the 1860s when Thomas Burberry started his own draper's business and developed a waterproof cloth that was hard-wearing, impenetrable to rain, yet cool and light to wear. The story has it that although Burberry called the cloth gaberdine, the name was changed to Burberry by one of its most famous customers, Edward VII, who on rainy days simply called for his "Burberry".

By the early twentieth century Burberry raincoats had become standard outdoor clothing as well as offering specialist protection for sportsmen and explorers. The explorer Scott and his team, for example, wore specially designed Burberry windproof suits on their ill-fated Antarctic trip.

17

Chanel No.5 Perfume Bottle

Coco Chanel (1883–1971) launched her Chanel No.5 perfume in 1921. Although other couturières had marketed their own scents, they were generally based on easily identifiable floral fragrances. Chanel was the first fashion designer to create a completely artificial perfume, with an aroma that smelled only of itself.

The idea came about when she was told that a rare sixteenth-century manuscript had been unearthed that was purported to be written by René the Florentine – personal perfume-maker to Queen Catherine de Medici. The creation was a collaboration between Chanel and a perfumier named Ernest Baux. Baux's legendary concoction combined eighty different organic chemical ingredients. Like Chanel's dresses, the perfume was designed to look elegant, simple and expensive – the hallmark of classic chic. The bottle is almost severe in its clear-glass design. The bottle is free from decoration, with only the words "No.5", "CHANEL" and "Paris". Although Chanel No.5 has been the world's biggest selling perfume range, it has managed to retain an air of exclusivity.

Bauhaus School Building

DATE: 1926
Dessau, Germany
ARCHITECT: Walter
Gropius (1883–1969)

From 1919 to 1928, Walter Gropius was the director of the most famous design school of the twentieth century – the Bauhaus. The School building that Gropius designed remains one of the seminal buildings of the Modern Movement. As its director, Gropius was responsible for establishing a new approach to design education, an approach that still influences the way design is taught. It set out a common foundation year from which students moved on to specialize in the design area of their choice.

Within the building itself, the elements of the course were expressed in a series of distinct areas connected by single-storey blocks. Different activities were expressed by a different treatment of the façade. For example, the workshop block used a reinforced concrete frame, hence the curtain wall, which wraps around the corner to reveal what goes on inside. The interior was equally important, most notably Gropius' office and the lecture theatre, which featured folded canvas and steel chairs by Marcel Breuer.

DATE: c.1926
DESIGNER: Marcel Breuer (1902–81)
MATERIAL: chrome-plated steel, wood and cane
MANUFACTURER: Gebrüder Thonet, Frankenberg, Germany

Cesca Chair

Marcel Breuer started his career at the most famous design school of the twentieth century – the Bauhaus in Germany. Enrolled in 1920, Breuer spent most of his time in the cabinet-making workshop. Almost immediately his work was recognized as highly original.

The story of how he discovered bent tubular steel has become part of the mythology of the Modern Movement. Legend has it that Breuer purchased an Adler bicycle and was so inspired by its strength and lightness, that he determined to apply the same techniques to furniture. Although many other designers experimented with the idea of a single, curved chair shape that did not use traditional legs, it was Breuer's B64 – nicknamed in the 1960s after Breuer's adopted daughter, Francesca – which became the decade's most-famous cantilevered design.

Breuer started to design buildings after he left the Bauhaus in 1928. His streamlined, continuous, flowing metal furniture informed his interiors and structures and became the perfect expression of Modernism.

E.1027,
Side Table

DATE: 1927
DESIGNER: Eileen Gray
(1879–1976)
MATERIAL: tubular steel
and acrylic glass
MANUFACTURER:
Atelier Eileen
Gray–Galerie Jean
Desert, Paris, France

In 1925, Eileen Gray and Jean Badovici designed a house – the Villa E.1027 near Saint Tropez – which featured furnishings made in her Paris workshops. Gray exploited new materials, such as the tubular steel used for the table shown here. It was originally designed as a bed table with the ring foot pushed under the bed for ease of use with adjustable tabletop height. It was later used as an occasional table for the living room.

The E.1027 Table relates to the cantilever chair experiments of the 1920s in that it also explored the idea of a table without conventional legs exploiting the streamlined possibilities of tubular steel. Gray, however, did not share the machine age preoccupations of many of her contemporaries in the European Modern Movement. Her driving force was less concerned with industrial techniques than with a search for visual perfection. The table was put into production again from the late 1970s.

DATE: 1927
MATERIAL: earthenware
MANUFACTURER:
T.G. Green
and Company,
Church Gresley,
Derbyshire, England

Cornish Kitchenware

Made from white earthenware dipped into blue glaze, the Cornish Kitchenware range was introduced by T.G. Green in 1927 to provide work for the factory's turners, whose jobs were then under threat because of the widespread economic slump. Originally consisting only of utilitarian jars and jugs, it was extended to include tableware such as mugs, plates and teapots. Aimed at the middle-income mass market, the range offered functional, cheap tableware for breakfast and informal meals. The title "Cornish" was a marketing strategy used to evoke farmhouse and country associations, while the use of blue reinforced the fresh feel of the dairy.

It became a British design classic, and early examples are avidly sought by collectors and featured in museums. In 1967 Royal College of Art graduate Judith Onions redesigned many of the Cornishware shapes and its commercial success continues.

Nord Express Poster

DATE: 1927
DESIGNER: Cassandre (1901–68)

Cassandre (the pseudonym of Adolphe Jean-Marie Mouron) was one of the best-known poster artists and type designers of the twentieth century. His great achievement was to bring the creative experiments of avant-garde movements such as Cubism into mainstream advertising. His technique employed a brilliant use of colour, powerful geometric forms and the integration of the company name with the image. Posters advertising trains and ships have become some of the best-known advertisements in the world. The agency that produced this work, and of which Cassandre was a founding partner, was the Alliance Graphique in Paris.

At the same time Cassandre designed typefaces for the old-established Paris-based type supplier Deberny and Peignot. His typefaces balanced Modernism with a fresh approach to letterforms, which became a deeply influential tradition. Cassandre restricted letterforms on his posters to capitals, believing that they enhanced the effect of the poster and allowed the type to be used on a large scale while remaining legible.

23

DATE: 1928
DESIGNERS:
Le Corbusier
(1887–1965), Pierre
Jeanneret (1896–1967)
and Charlotte Perriand
(1903–99)
MATERIAL: chrome
and painted steel
with leather and
fabric upholstery
MANUFACTURER: Thonet
Frères, Paris, France

Chaise Longue

During the mid- to late-1920s, some of the most talented European architects produced chair designs in tubular steel and leather that remain classic pieces of Modern furniture. Perhaps the greatest and most enduring piece of furniture produced at this time is the chaise longue designed in 1928, primarily by the French designer Charlotte Perriand, who is seen here lying on her creation in a photograph by Pierre Jeanneret.

The designs that were produced by Perriand, in collaboration with architect Le Corbusier and his cousin Pierre Jeanneret, are some of the purest expressions of the Modernist aesthetic, in which simplicity and function are the governing considerations. The feet of the chair mimic the profile of an aeroplane wing and establish the piece as an icon of the "machine age". Perriand's designs were first manufactured by Thonet and later by the Swiss company Embru. The chaise longue remains in production today in a modified form by Cassina.

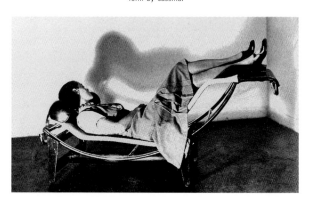

Barcelona Chair

DATE: 1929
DESIGNER: Ludwig Mies van der Rohe (1886–1969)
MATERIAL: chrome-plated steel with leather upholstery
MANUFACTURER: Bamberg Metallwerk-statten, Berlin, Germany, later Knoll Associates, New York City, USA

Mies van der Rohe designed the Barcelona chair for the German Pavilion at the 1929 International Exhibition in Barcelona. The German Pavilion was the only Modernist building in the exhibition and it created a sensation. Inside the austere structure, Mies displayed his famous chairs as if they were thrones for the Spanish king and queen; although it was designed within the Modernist aesthetic, the X-frame recalls medieval seats of power.

The chair was produced in America from 1948 and came to express modernity, taste and high quality, and signified the values of the mighty corporations to all who bought it. Mies had attempted to rethink furniture and seek out a dramatically different approach to the prevailing craft tradition. Both his architecture and his furniture evoked the machine. It suggested industry and engineering and the European admiration for *Amerikanismus*, the world of Henry Ford, of skyscrapers and new beginnings. Ironically, the Barcelona chair was the result of painstaking hand-craft techniques using traditional materials.

DATE: 1928–30
New York City, USA
ARCHITECT: William Van
Alen (1883–1954)

Chrysler Building

The Chrysler building is probably one of the most familiar buildings in the world. Indeed for many its opulent and dramatic profile has come to symbolize the Manhattan skyline. It was one of a number of high-rise buildings planned in the 1920s that established New York as *the* modern city of the twentieth century.

Although it was designed for the Chrysler motorcar company – its foyer was planned as a showroom and the exterior metal sculptural decoration evokes car grilles and emblems – the building was never used by Chrysler. During its construction, Van Alen was accused of financial impropriety and, whatever the truth, he never recovered his reputation.

Standing at 320 metres (1,048 feet), the Chrysler Building remains the most flamboyant example of Art Deco in New York's midtown district that saw so many corporations vying for attention, including the Woolworth building across the street and the Chenin Insurance headquarters on the opposite block.

Electric Light Bulbs Fabric

DATE: 1928–30
DESIGNER: S. Strusevich (active 1920s)
MATERIAL: printed cotton
MANUFACTURER: Sosnevsk Amalgamated Mills, Ivanava, Russia

After the Bolshevik Revolution of 1917, much emphasis was placed on the need for new imagery and products to convey the ideology of the Revolution to ordinary people. Russian Constructivist designers turned their attention to graphics, textiles and ceramics to express their vision of the future. The visual language of Constructivism was largely based on the use of multiple flat planes derived from Cubism. However, the Constructivists almost always insisted on an abstract and logical application of line and colour, and – the key element – the underlying suggestion of the Revolution's ideology. Each design carried a message to the people, represented here in the use of light bulbs as the repeat pattern illustrating the electrification programme of the Soviet Five Year Plan of 1928–32. The use of industry and technology as imagery symbolized a break with the bourgeois traditions of the nineteenth century.

Campbell's Soup Can

Joseph Campbell first began to can foods in 1869, in his factory in New Jersey. In 1898, he launched his canned soups with their characteristic red and white label. Campbell's were not the first company to use coloured labels on canned products; by the end of the nineteenth century they were used extensively in the USA. However, the design of the Campbell's can has endured, the soups were instantly popular and are still dominant in the American canned-soup market today. In fact they proved such an ubiquitous American product that in the 1960s Andy Warhol used the cans as a theme for a series of famous Pop Art paintings. Through his use of the product, packaging gained an important place in the history of twentieth-century art.

Leica Camera

DATE: 1930
DESIGNER: Oskar Barnack (1879–1936)
MATERIAL: plastic and metal
MANUFACTURER: Leitz, Germany

Small, quiet and discreet, in the 1930s the Leica camera produced a revolution. It was the first compact camera that could produce professional quality work and it quickly became the most popular photojournalistic camera in the world. Its origins go back to 1911 when Oskar Barnack joined the German engineering company Leitz. Barnack was trained as an engineer and an enthusiastic amateur photographer who started to work on prototypes for a small camera based on a simple idea: small negatives but big pictures. He produced prototypes of this camera and after World War One his boss Ernst Leitz decided to put it into production as the Leica. Their first camera was shown at the Leipzig Fair in 1925 followed by the Leica 1 in 1930, which was a new compact size and offered interchangeable lenses. These technological advances ensured that the Leica became the serious camera for professional photography in the 1930s.

DATE: 1932

DESIGNER:
George Carwardine
(1887–1948)

MATERIAL: lacquered
metal and Bakelite

MANUFACTURER:
Herbert Terry & Sons,
Redditch, England

Anglepoise Lamp

In the 1930s Britain produced a rational,
modern lamp for mass production, intended
as a functional light for both office and home.
The Anglepoise was designed for the Herbert
Terry company by George Carwardine, an
automotive engineer, and a director of Carwardine
Associates of Bath. His background is revealed in
the Anglepoise, which became one of the most
popular desk lights in the world. It was modelled
on the ergonomics of the human arm, with
springs instead of counterweights to hold the
arm in position. The lamp has sold for over sixty
years in enormous quantities and represents an
independent British tradition of rational design.

Glass Teapot

DATE: 1932
DESIGNER: Wilhelm Wagenfeld (1900–90)
MATERIAL: glass
MANUFACTURER: Jenaer Glaswerk Schott and Genossen, Jena, Germany

Although Wagenfeld went on to design electrical products for Braun in the 1950s, he is best known as a designer of glassware and ceramics. He studied at the Bauhaus – where he later taught – and remained a lifelong advocate of the principles of uncluttered simplicity and functionalism in design. Wagenfeld was teaching at the Berlin Kunsthochschule (art college) when he developed the tea service. It remains one of the purest expressions of Wagenfeld's industrial aesthetic, in which every aspect of the relationship between form and function is figuratively and literally transparent. Working with the same heat-resistant glass used to make test tubes, his brief was to design glassware, such as the teapot (shown here with a later cup and saucer) that could be used both in the kitchen and on the table. His pioneering use of new materials brought Bauhaus ideals to the mass-market.

DATE: 1932
DESIGNER: Aino Marsio-Aalto (1894–1949)
MATERIAL: pressed glass
MANUFACTURER: Karhula Iltala, Karhula, Finland

Pressed Glass 4644

Aino Marsio was the wife of the famous Finnish architect Alvar Aalto (see p.36). Like the wives of many other designers, her distinguished work has often been overshadowed by that of her more famous husband. Marsio was, nonetheless, a distinguished designer in her own right who also played a key role in Alvar's career, working in his office from 1924 until her death in 1949. Together they set up Artek, a company to market their designs.

Marsio enjoyed a long and successful collaboration with the glass manufacturer Karhula, beginning in 1932 when she won a design competition sponsored by the company to create a range of cheap, mass-produced pressed glass. Originally called *Bölgeblick*, the name of a café in the 1930 Stockholm Exhibition, the range included a pitcher, glasses, bowls, dishes and a creamer. It used thick glass made in three-piece moulds that left clear seams down the side. The distinctive "stepping rings" were not an original idea: in 1930 the Swedish designer Edvard Hald had used a similar technique for his Orrefors Glass Works bowls. Aino Aalto's glass went into production in 1934 and two years later won a gold medal at the Milan Triennale.

Marion Dorn Rug

DATE: 1932
DESIGNER: Marion Dorn
(1896–1964)
MATERIAL: wool
MANUFACTURER:
Wilton Royal Carpet
Factory Limited, UK

During the 1930s, Marion Dorn's rugs and textiles were the preferred choice of leading British Modernist architects who wanted furnishings sympathetic to their work. It was Dorn's rugs that appeared in Syrie Maughan's famous White Room at The Savoy Hotel, and in the foyer of Oswald P. Milne's redecorated Claridges Hotel, both in London.

Trained as a painter, Dorn's output was prolific. She designed fabric for the London Underground seats as well as fabrics, wallpapers and furniture. She was also commissioned to work on the great ocean liners of the period, including Cunard's *Queen Mary*. During the 1930s, she completed over one hundred rug designs for Wilton Royal, which led to her being described in the *Architectural Review* magazine as "the architect of floors". Her long and fruitful collaboration with Wilton concentrated on handmade rugs, usually produced in limited editions. Dorn's rugs were used in the new Modernist interiors to define particular spaces, often placed at key points with furniture arranged around the rug or left in isolation as a decorative feature. The patterns were generally bold geometric shapes but her use of colour was restrained, employing tones of white, cream, black and brown.

DATE: 1932
DESIGNER: Man Ray
(1870–1976)
CLIENT: London
Transport,
London, England

Poster for London Transport

Man Ray studied art in New York and worked across many different media, perhaps most notably photography. In 1939 he was invited to design a poster for London Transport. Man Ray actually produced two posters, one with the text "London Transport", the other with the copy "Keeps London Going", which were intended to be seen as a pair. Here the famous London Transport logo is transformed into a 3-D planet, which orbits around Saturn. London Transport therefore enters the firmament of the stars with its connections of speed, distance and the future. In this way Man Ray introduced to the British public the ideas of the Surrealist movement. The Surrealists experimented with ways of delving into hidden desires and memories through chance operations and automatic writing. The poster is an example of the way the fine art imagery of 1930s Surrealism filtered through to the world of advertising and graphic design.

LONDON TRANSPORT–

Poster for Shell

DATE: 1932
DESIGNER: Graham Sutherland (1903–80)
CLIENT: Shell Mex Limited, London, England

EVERYWHERE YOU GO

THE GREAT GLOBE. SWANAGE.   BY GRAHAM SUTHERLAND

YOU CAN BE SURE OF SHELL

Shell Mex was the name under which the international Shell Group ran its British marketing operation and in 1932 they appointed a new publicity director, J.L. Beddington. His insight turned the British Shell advertisements of the 1930s into one of the classic campaigns of the twentieth century. Shell used the advertisements on the sides of their lorries and in the press. They were intended to appear in series, and to change every few weeks with the aim of striking a blow against the use of ugly hoardings that many felt were becoming a blight in the countryside. It was Beddington who decided to use a range of leading Modernist painters to provide strikingly original images for their product. What made the Shell campaign so interesting was that it was a clearly directed series that attracted attention for the product via its association with the new, and then daring, art of painters including Graham Sutherland, who created this poster depicting the Great Globe at Swanage.

DATE: 1932–33
DESIGNER: Alvar Aalto
(1898–1976)
MATERIAL: plywood
MANUFACTURER: Artek,
Helsinki, Finland

Stacking Stool "L" Leg

Alvar Aalto's great achievement was the production
of designs that were simultaneously ahead of their
time and timeless. Designed as fixtures for his
buildings, the furniture reflects exactly the same
aesthetic as the architecture – they remain part
of the same vision.

The beauty of his plywood furniture meant
that it became more than just furniture – it was
appreciated and collected as sculpture for the
modern interior. In this context, for example,
his plywood kitchen stools were specified as
seating for Manchester's Hacienda nightclub
in the 1980s, by designer Ben Kelly, and for
kitchens, restaurants and homes all over the
world. Aalto's designs have found a place in
the modern domestic interior and inspired
countless imitations in stores such
as Ikea. Aalto's choice
of natural materials – such as
wood – and his simple use of
curves reflects both an interest
in organic forms and the need
for a human and humane
aesthetic.

In 1925 he married the
architect Aino Marsio (*see*
p.32), his most important
collaborator. It was she
who ran the Artek Wooden
Furniture company, which
marketed Aalto's designs
that found almost immediate
commercial success around
the world.

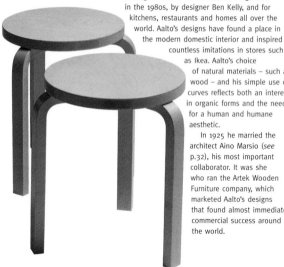

Dutch Post Office Graphics

DATE: 1934
DESIGNER: Piet Zwart
(1885–1977)

After World War One, Dutch designer Piet Zwart became involved with the *De Stijl* movement working for one of its leading architects, Jan Wils. Through him Zwart met an important client, N.V. Nederlandsche Kabelfabriek, for whom he began designing posters.

Zwart overturned the conventions of advertising by introducing the techniques of photomontage and random lettering. This work owes a debt to the experiments of Russian Constructivists whose work was published in the *De Stijl* magazine of the time. Although Zwart used the movement's preference for primary colours in his work, his approach was freer and more exuberant than the formalist tradition of Dutch graphic design. He introduced the ideas of the Dada group and their exploitation of elements of humour and irony. The appeal and originality of Zwart's work attracted the attention of the Dutch Post Office (PTT) and from 1929 he began a long collaboration with them, working on the design of stamps and other material.

DATE: 1934

DESIGNER: Wells
Coates (1895–1958)

MATERIALS: moulded
brown phenolic
Bakelite and
chromium

MANUFACTURER:
E.K. Cole Ltd, UK

Ekco AD 65 Radio

Wells Coates was a Canadian-trained architect who
came to London in the early 1920s and became
one of the pioneers of British Modernism.
He designed important buildings in the new
architectural style and it was inevitable that he
would attract the attention of manufacturers like
E.K. Cole, who wanted to modernize their industry.
Wells' Wireless Receiving Set AD 65 was the result
of a design competition held in 1932 by Eric K.
Cole to produce the ideal plastic radio. Wells
Coates' winning design was produced, with
variations, from 1934 until 1946 and became
a best-seller for the company. It was a radical
departure from traditional forms and materials
of radio cabinet construction. The AD 65 had
a distinctive circular cabinet of moulded brown
Bakelite made to fit a circular speaker.
The shape was reiterated in the
controls and arc of the channel
display and gave the radio
an entirely novel form
that also reduced
tooling costs.
A less expensive
and more popular
"walnut-look"
version of the
AD 65 was
also available.

Falling Water

DATE: 1935–37
Bear Run,
Pennsylvania, USA
DESIGNER: Frank Lloyd
Wright (1869–1959)

Frank Lloyd Wright was one of the great American individualists in architecture. He is important not only because of the quality of his ideas and buildings, but because almost single-handedly he created the idea of the architect as superstar. His architectural style changed throughout his career from decade to decade, almost from project to project. A common thread running through his work, however, is his attempt to create an organic architecture that has a dialogue with nature.

Falling Water exemplifies this concept and remains one of his most startling and original works. It was built for the Kaufmann family as a weekend retreat, on a site overlooking the Bear Run stream that the family wanted to be incorporated into the final design. The house is a mix of natural and man-made forms. Frank Lloyd Wright had observed that a high rock ledge beside the stream could be used to cantilever the house, so that it stood above the stream and at the same time could become almost part of it. Each cantilever has a balcony that overlooks the stream, bringing inhabitants into contact with water and nature: the whole house seems to merge with the landscape, its layers becoming the strata of the terrain.

DATE: 1937
DESIGNER: Russel
Wright (1904–76)
MATERIAL: glazed
earthenware
MANUFACTURER:
Steubenville Pottery,
East Liverpool,
Ohio, USA

American Modern Table Service

More than any other American designer, the work
of Russel Wright has come to represent an image
of informal living in the 1940s. He concentrated
on the design of homeware – particularly
tableware – and his American Modern service,
designed in 1937 and in production from 1939
to 1959, was a huge commercial success. It sold
over eighty million pieces, making it one of the
most popular tableware sets ever designed.

The American Modern also signalled a more
widespread change in American design. In the
1930s the work of Surrealist painters and
sculptors was widely exhibited in New
York. Their use of biomorphic shapes
had a gradual impact on design. At the
same time the leading American architect
Frank Lloyd Wright was shifting direction
towards a more natural architectural
form, exploring traditions and roots
of American visual culture. American
Modern brought these new ideas to
the public – the shape of the water
jug, for example, was compared
to a traditional eighteenth-century
coal scuttle, while other pieces
defined the new colour
and organic style
of the period.

Hudson J-3a Train

DATE: 1938
DESIGNER: Henry Dreyfuss (1903–72)
MANUFACTURER: New York Central Railroad, USA

In the interwar years designers and architects in Europe and America were gripped by the possibilities of speed and power afforded by modern technology. Streamlining, the practice of shaping an object to reduce drag, found its greatest expression in Henry Dreyfuss' locomotive for the New York Central Railroad. Dreyfuss opened his own industrial design bureau in 1929 and quickly become one of the leading exponents of a rational and functional approach to design that was characterized by clean lines and bold, undecorated statements in form.

During the 1930s in America streamlining developed into a superficial style that was applied to objects as diverse as cameras and vacuum cleaners. Dreyfuss was largely opposed to this practice, which he considered a rejection of pure functionalism and ergonomic or anthropometric design. His measured and integral approach resulted in some of the most enduring classics of twentieth-century product design such as his telephone for the American Bell Company in 1933 that defined the shape of the telephone for more than fifty years.

DATE: 1939
MATERIAL:
chrome plate
MANUFACTURER: HMV,
London, England

Bruton Reflective Electric Fire

To symbolize its qualities of modernity and efficiency, the designers of electrical products in the 1930s looked to reproduce features derived from Art Deco and streamlined automobile styling. The Bruton electric fire was typical of many designs of the period in that the extensive use of chrome had connotations of contemporary car styling. In addition, its use of a double parabola also improved the heat distribution and thus the efficiency of the fire.

The introduction of electric fires into the domestic market offered consumers their first experience of instant and portable heating in the home, and, although relatively expensive to run, were extremely popular supplements to coal fires, which were the standard form of heating before the widespread introduction of central heating in the postwar period.

Lucky Strike Cigarette Pack

DATE: 1942
DESIGNER: Raymond Loewy (1893–1986)

The majority of pack designs are not attributable to a single individual. Lucky Strike cigarettes is one exception. Raymond Loewy is an example of a famous designer working in the field of pack design. The brand was established in 1917 by the American Tobacco Company, founded by James Buchanan Duke. The red bull's-eye motif originated on the packaging of Lucky Strike Tobacco, which was already an established brand. In 1942 Loewy was commissioned to change the pack, his brief being to increase sales. He did this by introducing a white background (it was previously green). This strengthened and defined the pack's distinctive logo. The word "cigarettes" was placed in an Art Deco-style typeface, running across the bottom.

DATE: 1945
DESIGNER: Corradino
d'Ascanio (1891–1981)
MANUFACTURER:
Piaggio, Italy

Vespa

At the close of World War Two, like most European countries, Italy faced a transport crisis. The Piaggio company constructed aeroplanes but during the war the factory was bombed. The company's president Enrico Piaggio decided to replace aeronautic production with building a vehicle that was cheap, reliable, easy to maintain and easy to drive. Piaggio's chief engineer Corradino d'Ascanio set about designing a scooter that would be launched in 1946 as the Vespa, which is Italian for "wasp".

D'Ascanio brought his knowledge of helicopter and aircraft engine design to bear on the Vespa's development. He incorporated "stress-skin" technology with a body and frame fused into a unified whole. This monocoque design, now a staple of the automotive industry, was virtually unique in civilian vehicle design in 1945. As this 1960s photo demonstrates, the Vespa's surprising and stylish looks have made it an enduring favourite.

Wichita House

DATE: 1946
DESIGNER: Richard
Buckminster Fuller
(1895–1983)

Despite the fact he never completed any formal architectural training, Buckminster Fuller remains a seminal influence in twentieth-century design and architecture. In 1927 he invented a new house that he called Dymaxion, a word derived from the combination of the concepts of dynamism and efficiency. Using factory-built units, this startlingly futuristic house was Buckminster Fuller's model for technologically enhanced modern living. His approach was to have a profound influence on young architects in the postwar period.

The Wichita House, designed in 1946, is an extension of Buckminster Fuller's early ideas and provides a unique vision of his response to the machine aesthetic. Its use of factory components reflected the onset of the consumer age, the promise of the future and the potential of new technology. It was hardly surprising that Buckminster Fuller's experiments with geodesic dome structures and his extensive writings proved inspirational for a 1960s culture dedicated to the exploration of the future.

Dior: The New Look

On February 2, 1947, Christian Dior's collection was dubbed the "New Look" by American fashion editor Carmel Snow. Dior's designs cut straight across the social feelings and the fashion of the time. In 1947, the general mood was still towards austerity. Much of Europe lay in ruins and the process of rebuilding was a daunting programme. Many felt that during such a period Dior's look was inappropriate.

When Dior's extravagant dresses were shown on the catwalk, riots ensued: women wearing the clothes were attacked in the streets, while the American ambassador declared them "unpatriotic". Nonetheless, Dior had struck deep feelings – after the trauma of war, women wanted a moment of extravagance.

Interestingly, Dior chose to look back to the *belle époque* tradition of the 1880s for his inspiration, a style that saw the female body incarcerated in steel corsets and swathed in metres of material. It was ironic that Dior, from the rarefied world of Paris couture, produced the first postwar rebel look – one that developed into the rock and roll skirts of the 1950s.

46

La Pavoni Coffee Machine

DATE: 1947
DESIGNER: Gio Ponti (1891–1979)
MANUFACTURER: La Pavoni, San Giuliano, Italy

For the baby boom generation of the 1950s, two objects came to symbolize the new aesthetic of postwar Italian design: the Vespa scooter and the celebrated chrome espresso coffee machine, designed by Gio Ponti in 1947 for La Pavoni. Its sleek engineering styling was no accident. During the 1930s, Ponti was a rare Italian example of a product designer working for industry. He studied architecture in Milan and graduated in 1921. He was an influential writer and educator. In 1928, he became the founding editor of *Domus*, which he edited for fifty years, and for many years

Ponti taught at the Milan Polytechnic and helped shape the intellectual ideas underlying the best of Italian design.

La Pavoni exported its coffee machine all over the world but it was particularly important in London, forever associated with the new teenage lifestyle of coffee bars. It represented an important stylistic shift away from American dominance to an emphasis on things European and became part of a new outlook revealed in films like *The Ipcress File,* starring Michael Caine and novels such as *Absolute Beginners* by Colin MacInnes.

47

DATE: 1949
Pacific Palisades,
California, USA
ARCHITECT: Charles
Eames (1907–78)

Eames House

The name Eames is synonymous with furniture, but he also trained as an architect in the 1930s. In 1937 Eames was invited by Eero Saarinen to teach at the Cranbrook Academy of Art, then a small and unknown school, but with ambitions of becoming an American Bauhaus. Here Eames worked alongside the influential sculptor–designer Harry Bertoia, and met key figures such as Florence Knoll. This shaped his attitudes to both design and architecture and marked the beginning of his fascination with new technology.

Eames never ran an architectural practice, but Eames House provided the prototype for a few private commissions. It consisted of two prefabricated steel-frame units, bought from an industrial catalogue, divided by a patio space. These frames were painted grey with infill panels, some of which are constructed from opaque materials while others are painted in bright yellows, reds and blues.

Arabesque Table

DATE: 1949
DESIGNER: Carlo Mollino (1905–73)
MATERIAL: maple plywood and glass
MANUFACTURER: Apelli, Varesio and Company, Turin, Italy

Carlo Mollino enjoys a cult status among architects and designers. His father, Eugenio, was an architect and engineer who instilled in his son an admiration of all things modern. He introduced Carlo to stunt flying – the designs of much of his streamlined furniture clearly echo the wings of early planes. Of greater significance was Mollino's obsession with the erotic and the female body. His archive contained thousands of photographs he took of the female nude placed in what he called "bachelor rooms" – specially designed environments for which he designed furniture and fixtures.

Mollino designed the first Arabesque table in 1949 for the living room of Casa Orenga in Turin. The shape of the glass top was taken from a naked woman's back in a drawing by the Surrealist artist Léonor Fini, while the perforated table frame has a similar organic quality to the reliefs of the sculptor Jean Arp.

DATE: 1946–49
DESIGNER: Edward Young and Jan Tschichold (1902–74)

Penguin Book Covers

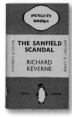

German-born Jan Tschichold emigrated to Switzerland in 1933. He became one of the most renowned typographers of the twentieth century, leading the new postwar developments in typography while remaining firmly committed to traditional Modernist principles. In 1923 Tschichold saw an exhibition of work from the Weimar Bauhaus and was converted to the principles of the Modern Movement.

The Penguin book covers, including the Penguin logo, were originally designed in the 1930s by Penguin's production manager, Edward Young. In 1946 Tschichold was employed by Sir Allen Lane, chairman of Penguin Books. Although he only worked for the publisher for three years, Tschichold introduced new standards of text layout and design that influenced the whole of British postwar graphic design. His achievement was to apply the theories of Modernism to the requirements of book production, with the establishment of the "Penguin Composition Rules".

Ericofon

The Ericofon was conceived as a lightweight and compact version of the standard two-piece telephone. Its sculptural form was startlingly original, its shape incorporating the ear piece, speaker and dial into a single unit. This was made possible by the new technology of miniaturization. Over the course of the following fourteen years the Ericofon developed through new versions that saw successive improvements in its engineering and its form. The gradual evolution of the product was led by the Blomberg team of designers over a fifteen-year period. Its commercial success was established in 1954 when the Ericofon became available in a series of bright colours. Ericsson was the first company to manufacture telephones in Sweden and it remains the largest.

DATE: 1949
DESIGNERS: Hugo Blomberg (born 1897), Ralph Lysell (born 1907) and Gösta Thames (born 1916)
MATERIAL: plastic and rubber
MANUFACTURER: L.M. Ericsson, Sweden

DATE: 1949–50
DESIGNERS: Charles
Eames (1907–78) and
Ray Eames (1916–88)
MATERIAL: plywood,
varnished steel,
fibreglass, masonite
and rubber
MANUFACTURER:
Herman Miller
Furniture Company,
Michigan, USA

Eames Storage Unit 421-C

The work of husband and wife Charles and Ray
Eames dominated postwar design both in America
and internationally, and their experiments with
new materials, particularly plywood and plastic,
established an aesthetic that came to express the
spirit of the 1950s. The Eames Storage Unit (ESU)
illustrated here uses steel-frame prefabricated
units with infill units painted in bright colours.
The idea was that by using prefabricated parts,
the user could assemble combinations according
to practical needs and personal taste. However,
self-assembly was a concept that 1950s people
found unappealing. Although the ESU inspired
many later copycat
versions, it was not a
commercial success.
Generally, however, Charles
and Ray Eames were
extremely fortunate in that
they acted as designers for
Herman Miller, America's
most prestigious furniture
company, who painstakingly
produced and marketed the
Eames furniture, which
featured then, as it does
now, in books, magazines
and high-profile interiors.

Tupperware

DATE: 1950S
DESIGNER: Tupperware
MATERIAL: plastic
MANUFACTURER:
Tupperware, Orlando,
Florida, USA

The American Earl Tupper first developed a range of containers made from polyethylene in 1945. Designed with air-tight seals to keep food fresher for longer periods of time, they revolutionized the storage of food in the home. The commercial success of Tupperware was based on the idea of home party-selling, which began in 1946 and was introduced to Britain in 1960.

The Tupperware range has been extended from basic kitchen storage and utensils to include cooking, table and picnic ware, and children's products – including toys. The designs are constantly updated to incorporate new fashions in shapes and colours.

Milk Bottle

Many British households still enjoy one of the world's most successful packaging recycling schemes – the doorstep delivery made possible by the milkman's round. First thing in the morning, milk is delivered in traditional glass bottles and the empty bottles are simply picked up, washed and reused. Originally the bottles were sealed with card, but these were replaced by aluminium tops during the 1930s. The bottle itself has evolved from a tall-necked vessel, shown here, to today's more compact and stocky bottle. Over the years the weight of the bottle has been steadily decreased without loss of strength, making a substantial saving in materials and energy.

Because the bottles are recycled and reused, the glass used to construct them must be capable of withstanding repeated use. The glass milk bottle is more than just packaging – it is linked to a valuable consumer service. Unfortunately the future of the traditional milk bottle is under threat, with increased use of supermarket plastic bottles and Tetra Paks.

Skylon

DATE: 1951
DESIGNERS: Sir Philip
Powell (born 1921)
and John Hidalgo
Moya (1920–94)

In 1945 Britain's new Labour Government supported plans by the Council of Industrial Design Industries, now known as the Design Council, to use design as a strategy in the regeneration of the postwar economy. Their most ambitious plan was a festival to mark the centenary of the Great Exhibition of 1851. The Festival of Britain was intended to show the British people a new future and provide an international forum to promote British design. Held on London's South Bank from May to September 1951, it was visited by over six million people.

With an aim of creating some memorable structures, the Festival committee commissioned the world's largest domed structure – the Dome of Discovery – and the world's tallest structure – the Skylon. Designed by two young architects, Philip Powell and John Hidalgo Moya, the Skylon towered over the site, its elegant and tensile structure creating an aesthetic that left a mark on a new generation of designers.

DATE: 1952
DESIGNER: Harry
Bertoia (1915–78)
MATERIALS: steel with
upholstery and rubber
MANUFACTURER:
Knoll Associates,
New York City, USA

No. 22
Diamond Chair

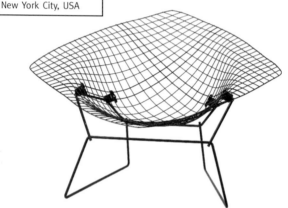

Many would argue that this is less of a chair than a piece of sculpture. It was designed to be viewed from all sides and extended Bertoia's earlier experiments with visual transparency. Certainly that was how he viewed his work. He had trained as a sculptor and shortly after designing this chair returned to that activity for the rest of his life. For many people, however, this wire chair has come to express the aesthetic of postwar design – new materials, a new lightness of form and a promise of the future.

From the late 1930s, when he moved to the Cranbrook Academy, Bertoia found himself at the centre of new American developments in design. At Cranbrook he met Florence Knoll who commissioned him to work on the chair of his choice. It took two years of production work to launch the Diamond range, using fabricated wire mesh to create a network of diamond patterns formed into these distinctive seating shells that float in space. Although they were Bertoia's last furniture designs, they remain classics.

P40 Reclining Armchair

DATE: 1954
DESIGNER: Orsaldo Borsani (1911–85)
MATERIAL: metal and upholstery
MANUFACTURER: Tecno, Milan, Italy

One of the most striking designs of the decade, this chair relies on an engineering aesthetic – with its adjustable seat and back, and flexible armrests, it resembles an aircraft seat. The chair was influenced by the techniques used in the automobile industry: foam rubber, then a new material from Pirelli, was used to pad the seat, the footrest was retractable and the chair could be adjusted into 486 different positions. Tecno, the manufacturer, started life as the Atelier Varedo, run by Gaetano Borsani, a progressive 1920s designer, who won a silver medal at the Monza Triennale of 1927. Borsani opened his first shop in Milan's prestigious Via Montenapoleone after the war. He later established Tecno, which was run by his two sons, designer Orsaldo and financial director Fulgenzio. Tecno concentrated on the design and production of furniture for offices and factories, including Olivetti.

DATE: shade 1954,
base 1962
DESIGNER: Isamu
Noguchi (1904–88)
MATERIAL: mulberry
bark paper, bamboo
and steel
MANUFACTURER:
Ozweki and Company,
Gifu, Japan

Model H Lamp

With this floor lamp, Isamu Noguchi explores the lamp shade both as a sculptural form and as a modern interpretation of the traditional Japanese paper lantern. In 1951, Noguchi travelled to Japan and studied these lanterns, known as *chochin*. Constructed from a framework of bamboo covered with paper, they were traditionally unornamented and used to diffuse candlelight. Inspired by their simplicity, Noguchi explored ways in which he could adapt them for electric light. Like *chochin*, Noguchi's lights were also designed to be collapsible, reflecting a widespread trend towards the purchase of consumer goods in flat packs. Using a mulberry bark paper, his lights could be folded into an envelope. Over twenty-five years he produced a whole series of designs based on the paper shades.

Routemaster Bus

DATE: 1954
DESIGNERS: A.A.M. Durrant (1898–1984) and Douglas Scott (1913–90)
MANUFACTURER: London Transport, London, England

The Routemaster, the classic red London bus, has become a symbol of Britain's capital throughout the world. Designed in 1954 to replace the existing trolley-buses, the Routemaster's ungainly appearance attracted criticism from many sceptics and, almost as soon as it entered service in 1959, its design was seen to be outdated, as legislation introduced in 1961 permitted buses of up to thirty feet (9 metres) in length. However, the Routemaster proved to be extremely popular with Londoners. In the 1970s London Transport's "Reshaping Plan" set out a timetable for the elimination of crewed vehicles such as the Routemaster in favour of new driver-only buses. However, this project proved to be both inefficient and unpopular, and as a result the Routemaster remains a part of London's cityscape after nearly forthy years of service.

DATE: 1955
Ronchamp, France
ARCHITECT: Le
Corbusier (1887–1965)

Notre-Dame de Haut

Associated with the purity of Modern Movement architecture, the expressive forms of the chapel at Ronchamp come as something of a surprise. Situated on the top of a hillside, the building's organic form dominates the site. Le Corbusier claimed that the dramatic roof-line's anthropomorphic form was inspired by a *"réaction poétique"* to a crab's shell he had originally picked up on a Long Island beach in the 1940s. For others it resembled the symbolic enclosure of a nun's veil.

Ronchamp was a project on which Le Corbusier lavished a great deal of personal attention. He wanted to create a place of peace and tranquillity, a religious and spiritual sanctuary. In this way Ronchamp exemplified a move away from his prewar work, which simulated the sleek lines of the machine by the use of pure form and white concrete. This building became one of the most accessible and popular examples of Le Corbusier's architecture. In some ways the techniques he used in the design of Ronchamp indicate a return to his very early work. This can be seen in his use of natural forms for the concave and convex walls and in the materials, which included the rubble of the destroyed church, which the chapel replaced, and reinforced concrete.

Ant Chair

DATE: 1955
DESIGNER: Arne Jacobsen (1902–71)
MATERIAL: moulded plywood and chrome steel
MANUFACTURER: Fritz Hansen, Denmark

Arne Jacobsen's achievement as an architect was to fuse the traditions of his native Denmark with those of mainstream Modernism. In common with many Scandinavian architects of his generation, Jacobsen also concerned himself with the design of the interior and its fixtures.

In 1952 he designed the Ant, a light, stackable chair, the seat and back of which were moulded from a single piece of plywood supported by a tubular steel frame. The chair was designed for the Fritz Hansen furniture factory. The Ant was Jacobsen's contribution to the language of modern, industrially manufactured furniture and it inspired a series of successors from 1952 to 1968 whose common elements were the continuous seat and back. The 3107 Ant Chair, pictured here, produced as the Series 7, was designed for the Rodovre Town Hall as a stacking chair. It is now manufactured in many different versions and numerous colours, and remains the most sold chair in Denmark.

DATE: 1955
DESIGNERS: Achille
Castiglioni (born 1918)
and Pier Giacomo
Castiglioni (1913–68)
MATERIAL: steel
MANUFACTURER: Gilardi
e Barzaghi, Milan, Italy

Luminator Lamp

The Castiglioni brothers made
a unique contribution to
Italian design in general but
to lighting design in particular.
In the postwar years of 1950s,
the light fitting assumed a
special significance in the
Italian quest to rebuild the
economy. Italian industry
needed to produce low-tech
objects for export for which
the added value of style
could command high prices.
The Luminator, with its low
manufacturing costs, was an
immediate success.

The Luminator was also
the first domestic light to
exploit the latest tungsten
bulb with a built-in reflector
on top. The lamp's visual
appearance, with its simple
vertical steel tube supported
on a slim tripod, reflects this
technical inspiration. The
Castiglionis' creation helped
to define the qualities of
postwar Italian design with its
use of stylish and expressive
sculptural form combining
good looks with function.

62

Seagram Building

DATE: 1954–58
New York City, USA
DESIGNER: Ludwig
Mies van der Rohe
(1886–1969)

Mies van der Rohe is one of the most influential architects of the twentieth century, whose buildings became the blueprint for a modern industrial society. Mies is famous for his ability to derive maximum effect from a minimum use of form, reflecting his legendary axiom "less is more".

On leaving his native Germany and moving to the USA, in 1938 he accepted a teaching post at the Illinois Institute of Technology, Chicago. Here he began to establish his distinctive architecture principles, using exposed metal frame structures to exploit bold rectangular forms. In the immediate postwar years his career acquired superstar status. Two of his skyscrapers – Lake Shore Drive Apartments, Chicago (1950) and the Seagram Office Building in New York (1954–58) – came to express the ambitions and spirit of America, inspiring the shape of hundreds of commercial quarters throughout the world.

63

DATE: 1959
DESIGNER: W.M. Russell
MANUFACTURER: Russell Hobbs, UK

K2 Kettle

Designed in 1959, the K2 was an advance on an earlier kettle of 1954, the K1, and part of a range that Russell Hobbs then called "Forgettable" because they included an automatic cut-off switch. This proved to be an extremely popular feature, because prior to its introduction, if the user forgot to turn off the kettle it simply filled the room with steam and burnt out the element. Other technical innovations included a powerful element that could bring the water to the boil in seconds and an indicator lever in the handle that automatically snapped back when it was turned off. The handle and lid knob were always cool to the touch. The K2 came in a variety of finishes from brushed and polished stainless steel to copper and chrome. In a market now dominated by the upright, electric plastic jug kettle the Russell Hobbs remains the leading metal kettle and has established itself as a classic.

"Anatomy of a Murder" Poster

DATE: 1959
DESIGNER: Saul Bass
(1920–96)

Bass is an American graphic designer best known
for his innovative work for the film makers Otto
Preminger and Alfred Hitchcock. A native New
Yorker, Saul Bass studied graphic design at night
school in Brooklyn College between 1944–45, while
practising as a freelance graphic designer. In 1946
he moved to Los Angeles and founded Saul Bass
and Associates. Bass designed more than sixty
graphic symbols for films and more than forty
movie title sequences. He is particularly well
known for his work with the director Otto

Preminger, for whom he
designed the symbols and
opening titles for *The Man
with the Golden Arm* (1955),
Bonjour Tristesse (1956) and
Anatomy of a Murder (1959)
and for his working
relationship with Alfred
Hitchcock, designing the
opening credits and,
some suggest, directing the
shower sequence, from
Psycho (1960).

From Hollywood's earliest
days until the mid-1950s,
credits to mainstream
American movies had been
set in virtually uniform
templates and superimposed
over an unchanging static
image or the film's
introductory scene. Bass used
animation and, later, live
action to create graphically
considered title sequences
that attracted the attention of
audiences and critics and
were soon widely imitated.

DATE: 1959
DESIGNER: Alec
Issigonis (1906–88)
MANUFACTURER:
Morris (British Motor
Corporation), UK

Mini

Like the skirt of the same name, the Mini has
come to be seen as a cultural icon of the 1960s,
a decade that saw a radical democratization in
British social life, spurred largely by the growth
of a new class of young, financially independent
people. The resulting dramatic increase in car
ownership led to the need for a small, dependable
car that conveyed an urban and youthful image.

The Mini represented a radical departure from
all previous car design. Issigonis produced an
extremely small car that could comfortably seat
four adults and was ideally suited to busy city
streets. The large amount of space in the car's
minimal interior was achieved by Issigonis
installing the engine transversely, or sideways.

With various modifications and new models,
such as the Mini Cooper, shown here starring in
the film *The Italian Job*, the Mini has been in
production for over thirty-five years and is
Britain's most successful and best-loved car.

TWA Terminal Building

DATE: 1956–62
John F. Kennedy
Airport, New York
City, USA
ARCHITECT: Eero
Saarinen (1910–61)

During the 1950s, Eero Saarinen helped to establish an original American architectural style that combined the European tradition with sculptural organic forms. Saarinen was responsible for some of America's best-known buildings, including the TWA terminal at John F. Kennedy Airport with its dramatic roofline. Through a daring use of concrete, Saarinen wanted to restore to architecture a new expression of form and excitement that would contrast with the anonymity of the high-rise building.

Although the Saarinen family emigrated to America in 1923, Eero returned to Europe to study sculpture – a training that was to have an important influence on his later work. When his father became Director of Architecture at the famous Cranbrook Academy, near Detroit, Eero came into contact with America's most progressive designers, including Florence Shust and Charles Eames. From 1937, Eames and Saarinen collaborated on a series of furniture projects using plywood.

From 1950, Saarinen's work with his partner Cesar Pelli developed a more inventive style. These buildings include the TWA terminal, with its distinctive parabolic arches that evoke wing forms, and Dulles Airport, Washington D.C. In London's Grosvenor Square, a late Saarinen collaboration with Yorke, Rosenberg and Mardall can be seen in the United States Embassy building.

DATE: 1964
DESIGNER: George Nelson (1907–86)
MATERIAL: aluminium, steel, wood, plastic and leather
MANUFACTURED: Herman Miller Furniture Company, Michigan, USA

Action Office

Herman Miller was America's most prestigious postwar furniture company. Their ambitious agenda for furniture design included a research department established in 1960 to introduce a new approach to the design of office furniture. George Nelson, the company's director of design from 1946–66, was given the brief to design a new system of modular units that could be adapted to the different requirements of people and work. The Action Office consisted of a chair on wheels, different tables and stackable shelf sections accompanied by a variety of accessories. The common component was the aluminium base, which acted as a support for the different units. In the 1960s Nelson was a pioneer is developing office systems that suited the new flexible work environments of the large company or small office. Although it was later promoted in a simplified form, the Action Office established a new standard for the design of office furniture and proved very popular.

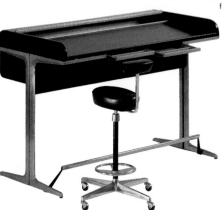

Mini-Skirt

Whether it was actually invented in London is not clear, but what is certain is that the mini-skirt came to represent the image of London's Swinging Sixties and became the most popular expression of a new relaxed attitude to the body.

Jean Shrimpton, shown here at the Melbourne Cup in 1965, caused a sensation when she appeared to present the fashion prize to the best-dressed lady attending the race meeting. In contrast to the prevalent dress codes, the "Shrimp" came hatless, gloveless and minus stockings, as well as wearing a mini.

The mini also represented some fundamental changes in fashion retailing. When America's *Time* magazine published its famous map of London in 1964 it did not illustrate the historical sites of interest but the new boutiques of Carnaby Street and Kings Road. These independent fashion outlets, including *Granny Takes A Trip*, *Hung On You* and *Lord John*, challenged the dominance of the more traditional fashion retailers. The most famous of these shops was Mary Quant's *Bazaar*, opened in 1957.

Air France Poster

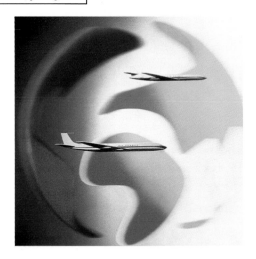

More than any other graphic designer, the work of Roger Excoffon came to define postwar French style. Best known as the designer of freeform typefaces in the 1950s, in the 1960s Excoffon moved away from the flamboyance of his earlier work with the design for the typeface Antique Olive, now called Nord. It was a move he acknowledged as a commercial decision, prompted by the demand from French printers for a clean 1960s feel.

Antique Olive started life in the late 1950s as a prototype upper case face for the Air France logo. With his assistant Gerard Blanchard, Excoffon

embarked on a serious research programme reading all the literature and research they could find on legibility and the psychology and impact of reading. They came to the conclusion that the upper half of the letters are the most important in word recognition and Excoffon therefore emphasized that aspect of the new face's character. Antique Olive was hugely popular and is largely credited with revitalizing the sans serif letter forms. Typical hallmarks of the Excoffon style included the use of off-register or double printing and interesting use of colour.

Mother and Child Graphics

DATE: 1966
DESIGNER: Herb Lubalin (1918–81)

In the postwar years, New York City became the world's cultural capital and one of the city's achievement's was the emergence of a distinctly American school of typography. If European typography was theoretical and structured then American typography was intuitive and informal, with a more open, direct presentation.

Born in New York City of immigrant Russian and German parents, Herb Lubalin studied typography at the Cooper Union School of Architecture. He led the way in manipulating typography to express an idea; letter forms became objects and images, and his figurative typography allowed visual properties a new freedom and importance. One of his most famous inventions was a new genre called the "typogram", a kind of brief visual poem. Perhaps the best-known example of this expressive typography is a masthead, designed in 1966, for a magazine called *Mother and Child* in which the ampersand evokes the image of the womb complete with foetus. These experiments, using what Lubalin called "the typographic image", were widely imitated in advertising. Designers realized the possibilities of using typography to create a "word picture" that allowed them a new creative potential.

It was Lubalin's achievement to pack an idea into a single, convincing piece of typography.

DATE: 1967
DESIGNER: Arne
Jacobsen (1902–71)
MATERIAL:
stainless steel
MANUFACTURER:
A.S. Stelton, Denmark

Cylinda Line
Tea Service

Arne Jacobsen's range of utility objects in stainless
steel conformed entirely to Modernist principles of
beauty through honesty to materials and method
of manufacture, while at the same time being
inexpensive and available to the mass of the
populace.

The Cylinda Line series – all based on the form
of a cylinder – was developed with Stelton over a
three-year period. The range included saucepans,
ice tongs, ashtrays and coffeepots.

Family Dog Poster

DATE: 1967
DESIGNER: Rick Griffin
(1944–91)

In the 1960s the arrival of Pop Design challenged the traditions of Modernism. Pop Design was instant, expendable, witty and ironic. Based in the Haight Ashbury district of San Francisco, and active participants in the emerging counter-culture movement, designers such as Stanley Mouse, Rick Griffin, Victor Moscoso and Alton Kelley, created posters for bands with bright, clashing colours inspired by their experience of psychedelic drugs and Indian mysticism. Because they did not work for the mainstream, Madison Avenue world of advertising they were also free to break all the rules about legibility, clarity and communication. Influenced by the organic letter forms of Art Nouveau they created complex lettering, in which legibility took second place to the overall shape of the word. These posters were also intended to reflect the experience of the acid trip. Certain elements were picked up by the mainstream, such as hand-drawn type and colour, but the real impact and revival of these posters was to be seen in the 1980s and 1990s.

DATE: 1967
DESIGNERS: Sir
Archibald Russell
(1904–95), Dr William
J. Strang (born 1921),
Pierre Satre (born
1909) and Lucien
Servanty (born 1909)

Concorde

Jointly developed by British Airways and Air France, Concorde was the first and remains the only supersonic civilian aircraft to be put into commercial service. Designing an aeroplane that could propel passengers at speeds exceeding that of sound involved surmounting thousands of individual technological and physical problems and resulted in a machine that looked more like a military aircraft than a civilian one.

Concorde has a novel shape, consisting of a needle-shaped nose and a "delta wing", both responses to the aerodynamic problems of flight at such high speeds. The distinctive wing shape combines great length and a minimum relative thickness that is well suited to supersonic flight as well as the lower speeds for take-off and landing. It also contributes great structural rigidity to the slim fuselage. The long, pointed nose assures maximum air penetration. The first test flights of the British and French prototypes began in 1969; commercial flights were introduced in 1976.

Galvez House

DATE: 1968–69
Mexico
DESIGNER: Luis
Barragán (born 1902)

Inspired by traditional Mexican architecture, Luis Barragán's work is notable for its use of intense colours. By fusing elements of Modernism with references to the vernacular architecture of his childhood, Barragán has succeeded in creating a series of memorable buildings of atmosphere and spirituality.

Because of the climate, Mexican architecture focuses upon the interior. Barragán often uses series of platforms leading to heavily walled interiors. Spaces are defined by walls and accentuated by use of light. By the careful placing of top lights and windows, Barragán frequently manipulates the projection of light onto walls. Colour is used to add a spiritual dimension to the interior and further define the space. Barragán's individual palette often includes deep rich reds, acid tones of yellow, green and pink. It is his use of colour which has so deeply influenced the work of many contemporary interior designers. Traditional vernacular devices are balanced with Barragán's love of the abstracted forms of Modernism. The effect of Barragán's work has been compared to the balance and stillness of a De Chirico painting – it is always emotionally charged, offering a sense of refuge and memory.

DATE: 1969
DESIGNERS: Marco Zanuso (born 1916) and Richard Sapper (born 1932)
MATERIAL: plastic and glass
MANUFACTURER: Brionvega, Milan, Italy

Brionvega Black ST/201

Brionvega is an Italian company with a long tradition of commissioning leading designers to give a distinctive form to its products. In the 1960s it was also one of the few international companies whose products stood out in contrast to the prevailing simple white aesthetics of the German Braun company and their Japanese imitators. The black 201 television set was designed by Marco Zanuso and Richard Sapper in 1969, continuing a partnership established in the early 1960s to develop a new generation of television sets and radios. More than any other object, this television represents the most uncompromising movement towards minimalism in 1960s Italian design. It defined the idea of the mysterious black box, emphasized by making the screen only visible when the television was switched on. The positioning of the controls on top of the set contributes to the sleek lines, making the 201 a novel form for a familiar appliance. It quickly became a cult object.

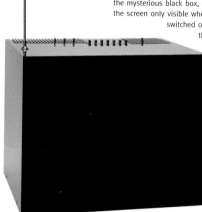

3089 A.B.C. Graduating Table Bowls

DATE: 1969
DESIGNER: Enzo Mari (born 1932)
MATERIAL: plastic melamine
MANUFACTURER: Danese, Milan, Italy

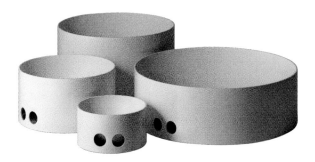

Until the 1960s, plastic had a negative image, as a material of little value. However, young designers of the decade did not see plastic as a cheap alternative for more expensive materials but an opportunity for strong colour and form, which helped to create the new aesthetic of Pop. Manufacturers were keen to exploit the market for new plastic goods and one example was the Italian company Danese. Founded by Bruno Danese in Milan in 1957, the company specialized in small household goods such as glasses, bowls and vases. Enzo Mari worked for Danese from its beginning and, in 1964, he produced a series of objects, including desk accessories and vases, that helped to define the company's reputation for stylish innovations in plastic.

Interested in semiology, Mari's book analyzing design as a linguistic system, *Funzione della ricerca estetica*, was published in 1970. Mari's approach to plastic design was technologically inventive and original, demonstrated here in a series of cylindrical table bowls with a concave central well, incorporating pierced holes on each side. In 1972 the bowls were included in a seminal exhibition on Italian design at the Museum of Modern Art, New York called "Italy: The New Domestic Landscape".

DATE: 1970
DESIGNER: Mario Bellini
(born 1935)
MATERIAL: plastic
MANUFACTURER:
Brionvega, Milan, Italy

Totem Stereo

In the 1960s miniaturization and more sophisticated technology suggested a new approach to sound system design – reduction to pure geometric form. One of Italy's most innovative firms, Brionvega, combined minimalism with fun and playfulness, stressing the sculptural potential of the object. It maintained a close relationship with avant-garde Italian designers in the 1960s and 1970s, and commissioned Totem from Mario Bellini whose inventive electronic equipment includes work for Olivetti. Totem was a directional design with speakers rotating out on a pivot to reveal the hidden record deck. When closed it formed a simple white cube that conceals its function.

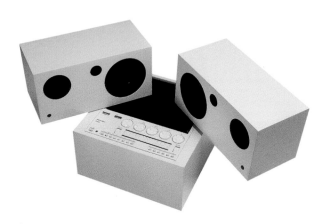

Tizio Table Lamp

DATE: 1972
DESIGNER: Richard Sapper (born 1932)
MATERIAL: ABS plastic and aluminium
MANUFACTURER: Artemide, Milan, Italy

Richard Sapper trained as an engineer in Munich and began his career working for Daimler. He went on to apply these technical skills to consumer products for companies such as Artemide and IBM. In the 1960s he worked on ground-breaking products for the television and radio manufacturer Brionvega. His approach promoted the idea that the technological function of a product should determine its appearance, and the Artemide Tizio lamp follows this principle. It is classic Sapper: finished in matt-black aluminium, the lamp has a formal beauty that incorporates balanced, lightweight engineering forms to produce an elegant shape with arms that move smoothly and offer a number of different, stable positions. It is also a technical success in that it uses a low-voltage halogen bulb, which gives a concentrated light source. The Tizio became one of Artemide's best-selling designs and won the Compasso d'Oro prize in 1979.

DATE: 1973
DESIGNER: Jakob
Jensen (born 1926)
MATERIAL: wood
and aluminium
MANUFACTURER:
Bang and Olufsen A/S,
Copenhagen, Denmark

Beogram 4000 Turntable

In 1944 Bang and Olufsen launched the revolutionary Grand Prix 44 RG, a compact cabinet incorporating a record player and a radio. In 1968 the Danish designer, Jakob Jensen, was placed in charge of Bang and Olufsen's hi-fi design programme. His vision for the company was simplicity and elegance. Jensen's anonymous and discreet styling for Bang and Olufsen has come to define the aesthetics of high-quality contemporary sound systems. Using state of the art technology with its precision components and electronic tangential arm, the Beogram was a rare example of a product from a European electronics company capable of holding its own in an industry dominated by the new Japanese companies. Bang and Olufsen continue to produce outstanding audio-visual equipment for the domestic market.

Sydney Opera House

DATE: 1956–73
Sydney, Australia
ARCHITECT: Jorn Utzon
(born 1918)

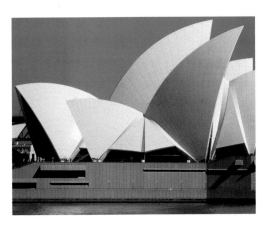

The Sydney Opera House has become one of the most famous buildings in the world. Jorn Utzon, a Danish architect, won the competition to design a new opera house for Sydney in 1957. Previously he had worked for Alvar Aalto from whom he learned an organic approach to architecture. His other inspiration was the work of the American architect Frank Lloyd Wright. Utzon's winning design was both functional and symbolic, housing two concert halls and public spaces. Its form evoked both the sea, which provides the dramatic backdrop for the building, and the graceful form of sea birds. In

this way the design marks a transition in twentieth-century architecture away from the geometry of early Modernism to a more expressive, sculptural approach to building.

Between 1956 and 1966, Utzon was responsible for the main structure of the building, but it was the engineer Ove Arup who enabled him to realize the ambitious form of the roof. Utzon chose to make the roof the focal point of the design because it was the feature most people would see. In this way, the concert hall, covered by the famous "prow-like" roof, became a sculpture – a fifth facade to the building.

DATE: 1971–76
Paris, France
ARCHITECTS: Richard
Rogers (born 1933)
and Renzo Piano
(born 1937)

Pompidou Centre

The Centre National de
l'Art et de la Culture Georges
Pompidou is an arts complex
that has become one of the
most famous and best-loved
buildings in Paris. To increase
the internal space, all the
services, air-conditioning pipes
and ducting of the building
were placed on the exterior.
The most dramatic feature
is the escalator with its
transparent covering
dominating the main facade,
which takes people into the
building. The effect of the
brightly coloured blues, reds
and greens resembles, in
Rogers' own words, "a giant
Meccano set".

The Centre proved a
brilliant solution to a complex
brief, which demanded a
library, galleries, a museum
of modern art and a research
centre. The internal spaces are
completely free of supports,
permitting maximum flexibility.
This was the first "museum"
not to be designed as an
imposing monument in the
nineteenth-century tradition,
but as a flexible framework
for cultural activity.

Sony Walkman

DATE: 1978
DESIGNER: Sony Design Centre
MATERIAL: plastic
MANUFACTURER: Sony, Tokyo, Japan

Sony chairman Akio Morita is said to have conceived this portable stereophonic cassette player whilst playing tennis, imagining a lightweight, easy-to-carry device for listening to music at any time. The Sony Walkman represents key changes in the 1970s and 1980s consumer markets. One of the first personalized products, both fashion accessory and functional object, the concept used existing technologies in an innovative and revolutionary way with new styling. With about fifty million sales, the Walkman has seen many versions, such as the model shown here. It continues to evolve in line with social and fashion trends and the need for individual customization.

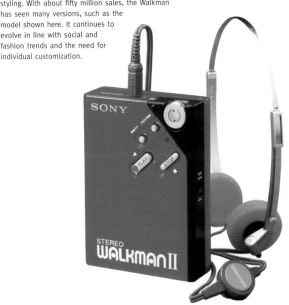

DATE: 1980
DESIGNER: Gae Aulenti
(born 1927)
MATERIAL: glass, metal
and rubber
MANUFACTURER:
Fontane Arte,
Milan, Italy

Table With Wheels

Gae Aulenti remains a rare phenomenon: a female designer. Trained as an architect in Milan, she made her greatest impact as an exhibition designer but worked on other projects including a collaboration with Richard Sapper in 1972 on a proposal for new urban transportation systems, presented at the 1979 Milan XVI Triennale. Working from the 1950s she enjoyed a quiet profile, admired for her furniture designs and commissions for interiors and showrooms for Knoll, Fiat, Olivetti, and Pirelli. Then she was chosen to design the new Paris museum Musée d'Orsay, which was sited in an old railway station. The brilliant success of this project placed her in the international design spotlight. Gae Aulenti's work reveals a complex sensibility, wishing to make contemporary objects rational, yet also accessible and human. The coffee table is one of her most famous designs using industrial components. The wheels form the base for a more traditional glass table top.

Carlton Sideboard

DATE: 1981
DESIGNER: Ettore Sottsass (born 1917)
MATERIAL: wood and plastic laminate
MANUFACTURER: Memphis, Milan, Italy

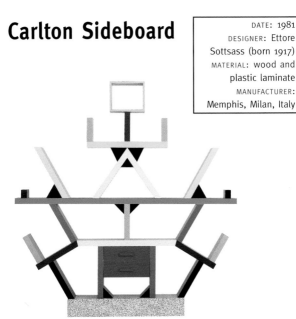

In 1981, Ettore Sottsass, one of Italy's best-known designers, launched a new design group in Milan. Rather tellingly, it was called Memphis – the home town of Elvis Presley and the sacred capital of the Egyptian Pharaohs. Memphis was an immediate success. Set against the prevailing late-1970s mood for the "classic" and "good taste", Sottsass and his collaborators produced something exciting, fresh and new. Their furniture used a new palette of colours and materials, mixing plastic laminates with expensive wood veneers in bright reds, blues and yellows. These objects used references to the past, reworking the coffee bar era of the 1950s. Memphis challenged basic assumptions: for example, why should the shelves of a bookcase be straight?

The Carlton Bookcase is one of the most famous of the Memphis objects. Like so much of Sottsass' work, the piece combines his interest in Indian and Aztec art, 1950s popular culture and his roots in 1960s Pop.

Dyson Dual Cyclone

DATE: 1983

DESIGNER: James Dyson (born 1947)

MATERIAL: moulded plastics

MANUFACTURER: Dyson Appliances, UK

Since it was first produced for the mass market in 1993 the Dual Cyclone, which combines unconventional styling with technical innovation, has become a best-selling vacuum cleaner. Conventional cleaners use a filter bag, which traps dirt and dust while allowing clean air to re-enter the room. The effectiveness of such cleaners reduces as the bag fills up. James Dyson's cyclonic system, using the principle of centrifugal force, sucks up air and revolves it at high speed through two cyclone chambers until the dust and dirt drop to the bottom of the transparent cylinder.

Dyson spent five years and over five thousand prototypes developing his first cleaner, a very Postmodern pink and lavender machine called the G-Force. In 1984 a Japanese company put it into limited production, and in 1991 Dyson sold his licence interests to the Japanese, which enabled him to fund the manufacture and marketing of the cleaner in Britain.

Swatch

DATE: 1983
MANUFACTURER:
Swatch, Switzerland

The watch market has been transformed by Swatch
since the 1980s. The combination of Swiss
technology, design and low price has meant that
the Swatch became the fashion accessory of the
1980s. Its first watch, with a black plastic strap
and plain watch face, has become the classic style.
Adopting the marketing principles of the fashion
industry, the company produces collections every
season, limited editions for dedicated collectors,
and a range of classic designs that are kept in
production. Throughout the twentieth century,
watch design has always reflected fashion, but
over the last fifteen years the company has
produced a range of styles and colours that have
turned the company into a world leader.

Early prototypes were designed by three
engineers, Ernst Thonke, Jacques Muller and Elmar
Mock. They developed the first integrated watch,
in which the action was not a separate element.
Then came the quartz Swatch, which overcame the
association of plastic with unreliability, by offering
the consumer the latest technology. Composed
of fifty-one pieces as opposed to over ninety in
traditional watches, Swatch also made a virtue of
these workings by producing a transparent version,
in which the components were fully visible.

DATE: 1984
DESIGNER: Ingo Maurer
(born 1932)
MATERIAL: glass,
ceramic, metal
and plastic
MANUFACTURER:
Design M Ingo Maurer,
Munich, Germany

Ya Ya Ho
Lighting System

Such was the originality of
Ya Ya Ho that it turned the
German designer Ingo Maurer
into an overnight success.
The light became his
signature piece and it was
hailed as one of the freshest
and most original lighting
designs of the decade. Ya Ya
Ho stretched out fine wires
of low-tension cabling onto
which were attached halogen
lamps, counterbalanced
to create the effect of a
sculptural mobile. The clip-on
light sources can be arranged
by the consumer at will.

Maurer exploited the 1980s
development of the halogen
family of bulbs and the new
mini fluorescent lamps. He
wanted to promote a situation
where lighting could be
reduced to a series of simple
components offering a wide
variety of designed forms and
lighting effects, using low-
voltage lighting sources that
enable the consumer to touch
and move the lights freely.

Hong Kong and Shanghai Banking Corporation

DATE: 1985
Central District,
Hong Kong
ARCHITECT: Sir Norman
Foster (born 1935)

Designed in 1979, this was Norman Foster's first skyscraper. The bank combined many of Foster's architectural preoccupations: his attempt to redefine the faceless office blocks associated with the Modern Movement; a concern with structure; the use of new materials and technology; and his introduction of natural light into the building. It occupies one of the most spectacular sites on the island, leading to the waterfront while the granite rock formations of Victoria Peak rise in the background.

The building is suspended from pairs of spectacular steel masts arranged in three bays, connected at key points by two-storey trusses from which the floor clusters are suspended. This staggered profile created interior spaces of varying width and depth, allowing garden terraces and dramatic east and west elevations. The combination of solid structure and transparent panels reveals the rich mixture of spaces within.

DATE: 1985
DESIGNER: Massimo
Morozzi (born 1941)
MATERIAL:
stainless steel
MANUFACTURER: Alessi,
Crusinallo, Italy

Pasta Set 9092

Established in the 1930s, the Italian company
Alessi enjoyed a reputation for good quality
metalware. In 1983 they launched a new and
hugely successful series of products for the home
called Officina Alessi. Alessi commissioned leading
international architects and designers to produce
specially designed, distinctive products exploiting
Alessi's traditional expertise in the use of stainless
steel, brass, copper and silver. In some ways the
choice of Massimo Morozzi was typical of the
Alessi approach in that previously Morozzi was
a leading Italian avant-garde designer, producing
radical and experimental work that did not make
him the obvious candidate for a pasta set.
Morozzi's set consists of a multi-purpose boiling
unit and steamer, a colander with handles and a
lid with a hollow knob for steam to
escape. Not only did it
succeed in cooking
large quantities of
pasta efficiently –
it also made a stylish
contribution to the
new "designer kitchen"
of the 1980s.

Whistling Kettle 9093

DATE: 1985
DESIGNER: Michael Graves (born 1934)
MATERIAL: steel with polyamide handle
MANUFACTURER: Alessi, Crusinallo, Italy

Michael Graves is one of the leading theorists and architects of Postmodernism, a movement in architecture and design that has sought to invest buildings and objects with a narrative content. He has become an influential spokesman for an approach to design that advocates bold use of colour and pattern and witty references to popular culture. In this respect he broke away from his original allegiance to Modernism and it is significant that when the Italian Memphis group produced their first collection in 1982 it featured the work of only one American: Graves. This brought him to the attention of Alessi.

The Graves kettle was one of Alessi's first, and most successful, experiments with Postmodernism. With its simple form and restrained use of materials, the kettle is essentially a straightforward modern piece of design. However, Graves gives it a humorous twist with the addition of a blue plastic bird mounted on the spout that sings when the water boils.

DATE: 1986
DESIGNER: Yohji
Yamamoto (born 1943)

Japanese Fashion Design

Until the beginning of the 1980s, the concept of Japanese fashion design in the context of the international market simply did not exist. Integral to the increasing awareness of Japanese fashion designers has been Yohji Yamamoto.

Yamamoto studied fashion in Tokyo under Chie Koike, who, having studied with Yves Saint Laurent, provided a link with the world of Paris couture. He developed a unique style that broke away from the predominance of closely fitted, tailored fashion, introducing a looser feel to the cut of clothes by draping and layering. Yamamoto's simple, minimalist effects relied on the quality and the feel of fabrics, which also made his clothes extremely difficult to copy. New and innovative fabrics have always been a touchstone of his work. He viewed clothes as sculptural pieces, their pleats and folds producing eye-catching forms that shaped the body in a way that was reminiscent of the traditional Japanese kimono but that was nonetheless perfectly relevant to a contemporary lifestyle.

Kidosaki House

DATE: 1982–86
Tokyo, Japan
DESIGNER: Tadao Ando
(born 1941)

Tadao Ando is one of Japan's most celebrated architects. Although much of his work, including this house, can be found in Tokyo, his practice is based in Osaka away from the pressures of city life. The Kidosaki House is a typical example of his philosophy. Located in a quiet suburb of Tokyo, Ando's design provides a home for three families, each with separate living spaces within the main volume of the house. The house itself is a perfect twelve-metre cube surrounded by a wall that runs along the perimeter of the site. The living room looks out through floor-to-ceiling windows onto a courtyard, which introduces an element of nature within the cityscape.

The interior is beautifully simple. Ando's concern is to reduce form to its essentials. He uses light to articulate and highlight form, reflecting both modern design and also traditional Japanese ways of living. One of the key themes in Ando's interiors is a rejection of the chaos of modern metropolitan life. His solution is to create haven-like interiors, often hidden away surrounded by walls and gardens, that offer the occupant a peaceful refuge.

DATE: 1986
DESIGNER: Neville Brody (born 1957)

The Face Magazine

Neville Brody is Britain's best-known designer and his work, in particular his Brody font, defined the graphic style of the 1980s. In 1976 Brody went to study graphic design at the London College of Printing (LCP), but he disliked its dedication to the Swiss Modernist orthodoxy. By 1979, the year he graduated, the Punk revolution was in full swing and Brody gravitated towards the clubs and magazine scene of London.

In the early 1980s, if you wanted to know what was happening in terms of new style trends you simply read two magazines, *i-D*, designed by Terry Jones, and from 1981 *The Face*, which was originally designed by Brody. Brody's ideas of page layout and type design seemed fresh, radical and innovative. He developed certain distinctive trademarks, using, for example, symbols and logo-type almost as road signs to guide the reader through the pages. Brody created a vocabulary for magazine design of the period using handwriting marks and type that ran sideways. This cover of *The Face* is the only issue that used only type and no cover photograph.

S Chair

DATE: 1987
DESIGNER: Tom Dixon
(born 1959)
MATERIAL: metal
and wicker

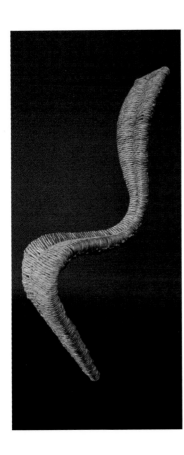

Tom Dixon was part of a group of young British designers in the 1980s who, inspired by the do-it-yourself aesthetic of Punk, started working with recycled materials and welded metal. These designs crossed the boundaries of sculpture, design and craft and became known as "creative salvage", a name Dixon chose for his first design company.

In the late 1980s Dixon began making more commercial designs, with creations such as the S chair. He based the distinctive organic curve of the chair on a sketch he made of a chicken. Over fifty different prototypes were made using many materials, including rush, wicker, old tyre rubber, paper and copper. In 1987, the well-known Italian furniture company Capellini bought the design and put it into mass production; since then it has been acquired by many leading international museums including the Victoria and Albert Museum in London and the Vitra Museum in Germany.

95

DATE: 1989
Weil-am-Rheim,
Germany
ARCHITECT: Frank Gehry
(born 1929)

Vitra Design Museum

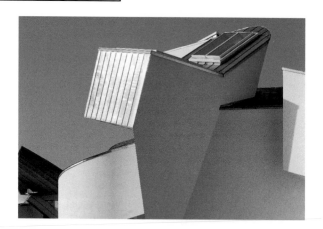

Frank Gehry's idiosyncratic, fun approach has made him America's best-known "fringe" architect. Almost single-handedly, he made this fringe not only mainstream but popular, with clients as diverse as the Disney Corporation and American universities. His approach helped to establish the meaning of the new Postmodernism.

Gehry invited the viewer or user to reassess their ideas and preconceptions about conventional objects. He used non-traditional materials, such as corrugated iron, chain-link fencing and pieces of wood, placed in surprising

contexts. Sculptural qualities help to define the effect of his buildings; they sometimes look as though someone has carved a deep curve into the wall, contrasting with a concave wall place alongside it. Gehry enjoyed close connections with the Pop Art movement, including his collaboration with Claes Oldenburg on the Santa Monica binocular building. These distinctive visual qualities made Gehry's work particularly appropriate for the design of art galleries, such as the Vitra Design Museum and the remarkable Guggenheim Museum in Bilbao.

Ty Nant
Water Bottle

In 1988 a new technique for colouring glass was introduced by a division of UK company British Foods under licence from an Australian research company, and in 1989 the stylish blue Ty Nant bottle appeared.

Ty Nant was the first modern packaged brand to use a distinctive colour of glass to add value and distinction in the highly competitive table water market. The company is one of the few manufacturers in the world that have successfully trademarked a colour–shape combination. The rich blue colour is similar to that of the "Bristol" blue glass introduced in the seventeenth century. Intended as a designer accessory, the Ty Nant bottle, with its extremely sensuous shape based on burgundy and champagne bottles, looked expensive and exclusive.

The distinctive style and strength of colour enables the consumer immediately to identify a product that would otherwise be inseparable from its contemporaries. In 1989 the bottle won the British Glass Award for Design Excellence. It has been marketed internationally and has proved very popular.

DATE: 1990
DESIGNER: Philippe Starck (born 1949)
MATERIAL: lacquered aluminium
MANUFACTURER: Vitra AG, Basel, Switzerland

WW Stool

Philippe Starck is now one of the best-known contemporary designers in the world. In the early 1980s, the project that brought him to public attention was a small Paris café near the Pompidou Centre called Café Costes. What was so interesting about the project was the fact that Starck designed all the fittings, including a three-legged chair, which became an international best-seller and has come to signify modern design in restaurants and venues all over the world.

Since then he has gone on to design many well-known objects, including his Juicy Salif Lemon Press for Alessi and the WW Stool, part of a series of designs that use anthropomorphic forms. The WW is a reference to the German film director Wim Wenders for whom he designed this office chair, defining the idea of a stool as a sculptural and growing form which resembles the roots of a living plant.

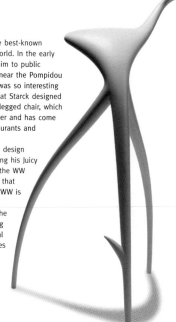

Ray Gun Magazine

DATE: 1990S
DESIGNER: David Carson (born 1958)

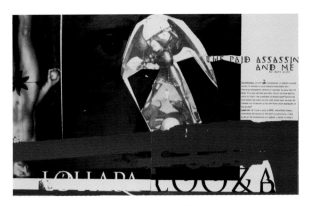

The American David Carson has become one of California's best-known graphic designers. His use of type and imagery and his work for *Ray Gun* magazine, which established his reputation, became highly influential in the 1990s. Carson is a self-taught graphic designer who originally studied sociology at university. Part of the Californian new wave, his work is based on magazine design, starting with *Beach Culture*, which has won over 100 awards worldwide for its innovative design. The American magazine *i-D* selected Carson as one of the USA's most innovative designers and he has maintained this profile with his more recent work for *Ray Gun*. This magazine for the visual arts rapidly achieved cult status for young graphic designers all over the world.

Carson no longer designs the magazine and has established his own design studio. His clients include Nike, Pepsi, whose 1994 campaign used a Carson type design, MTV, David Byrne, Kentucky Fried Chicken and Sony. Carson also works with Tony Kaye Films as a commercial and video director. He lectures worldwide on typography.

DATE: 1992
DESIGNER: David Mellor (born 1930)
MATERIAL: stainless steel and plastic
MANUFACTURER: David Mellor, Sheffield, England

Odeon Cutlery

David Mellor trained as a silversmith in his native Sheffield and then at the Royal College of Art in London. During the 1950s and 1960s he designed street lighting, bus shelters, road traffic signs and a pillar box for the Post Office. However, these contributions have been overshadowed by his importance as a designer, manufacturer and retailer of high-quality silver and stainless steel. In 1970, Mellor established his own factory at Broom Hall in Sheffield. From here he has directed every aspect of the design and production of his innovative cutlery. He has revolutionized the manufacturing process, introducing purpose-built machinery and a flexible work force in which each cutler is trained to carry out every stage of the production. Mellor has produced an exceptionally diverse range of cutlery designs, from the Embassy silver service, commissioned in 1965 for use in British embassies throughout the world, to a special service designed to meet the needs of the disabled.

Powerplay Armchair

DATE: 1992
DESIGNER: Frank Gehry (born 1929)
MATERIAL: high-bonding urea and laminated and bent maple wood strips
MANUFACTURER: Knoll Associates, New York City, USA

Frank Gehry can be placed in the great tradition of American individualist architects that includes Frank Lloyd Wright. His other trademark is the use of everyday materials in distinctly non-everyday ways – an approach which inspires his furniture design. Once again, the influence of the Pop aesthetic is important here. For Gehry, furniture should include the elements of surprise and challenge. The Powerplay chair reflects these ideas, and can be read as a cheeky reworking of his earlier design, the Wiggle – a cardboard version of the Rietveld Zig-Zag chair, which demystified a Modernist icon by using such a cheap everyday material. With the Powerplay Chair, Gehry uses bent wood.

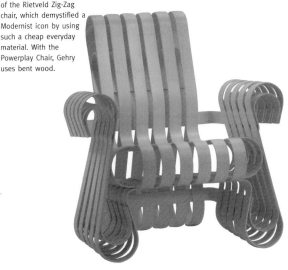

DATE: 1986–93
DESIGNER: Ron Arad
(born 1951)
MATERIAL: high-grade
sheet steel and
thumb screws
MANUFACTURER: Vitra
AG, Basel, Switzerland

Well Tempered Chair

Born in Israel, Ron Arad moved to London in 1973,
studied at the Architectural Association and in 1981
opened a furniture shop in Covent Garden. Called
"One Off", the showroom became a significant
part of the new British design wave of the 1980s
and established Arad as Britain's most creative
designer–maker. His early work used industrial
materials and recycled parts, notably the famous
Rover chair, which placed the car seat into a
tubular steel frame. Always an inventive maker,
Arad worked extensively in his metal workshop,
welding large pieces together to make installations
and furniture. Here Arad has reduced the
traditional armchair to simple folded forms
that challenge the conventional
idea of comfort and use.

Sardine Collector's Cabinet

DATE: 1995
DESIGNER: Michael Marriott (born 1963)
MATERIAL: MDF, sardine tins and wing nuts
MANUFACTURER: Space UK, London, England

In 1996 the Crafts Council in London put on an exhibition called "Recycling: Forms for The Next Century". As the title suggests the show explored the new interest in alternative design, in the reuse of materials and the search for a design future that took on board concerns for the environment and a less aggressive use of raw materials. This exhibition highlighted the work of Michael Marriott, a graduate from the furniture department of the Royal College of Art, whose quirky and fun objects caught the imagination of many people. His cabinet used a medium-density fibreboard structure to house used sardine cans as the drawers. This witty, simple and elegant solution suggested another agenda for design that looked back to the 1960s alternative tradition of Victor Papanek and the Whole Earth Catalogue.

In his work Marriott exploited the tradition of found objects. For him, found materials produced not only beautiful accidental effects but also established familiarity with the object. He recognized a culture with a wealth of wasted resources, and that he could capitalize on such materials with interesting qualities.

DATE: 1994
DESIGNER: Jasper Morrison (born 1959)
MATERIAL: plastic
MANUFACTURER: Magis, Treviso, Italy

Wine Rack

Jasper Morrison is a young British designer best known for his stylish, minimalist furniture, but he has also produced a series of objects for the home, including this new version of the wine rack. Previous designs had relied on traditional vernacular form, with wood and metal supports, sometimes scaled down for kitchen work surfaces. Jasper Morrison took the simple but obvious step of producing the wine rack in plastic. Using simple geometric forms he made it an accessory for the modern home, producing it in flat pack form in a series of bright modern colours.

Hannibal Tape Dispenser

DATE: 1990s
DESIGNER: Julian Brown
MATERIAL: plastic
MANUFACTURER: Rexite

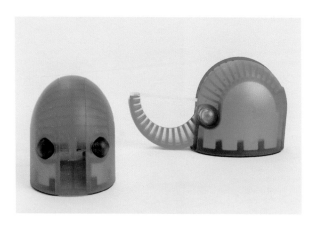

In 1998 Julian Brown received four international design awards for his tape dispenser, Hannibal. In December of the same year the American magazine *Time* included the object in its round-up of the best things of the year.

Brown started his career training as an engineer but switched to design and worked for a number of large practices before starting his own company, Studio Brown. Hannibal reflects his painstaking research and an empathy with product design that transforms what could have been a throwaway object into a design that is seen by many to represent style and direction in the late 1990s.

Rexite had made high-quality desk accessory ranges but they had not yet addressed "nomadic work tools", products that deliver a secondary function but are not location specific. The elephant idea was not whimsy but the result of careful research and study, the shape of the trunk perfect for the requirements of the dispenser. Not only could you open the trunk but it also could be configured to close again and keep the tape "dust free" ready for the next use. Rexite also went to extreme lengths to maintain the highest quality of tooling and manufacturing detail.

DATE: 1990S
DESIGNER: Vivienne
Westwood (born 1941)

Vivienne Westwood

Vivienne Westwood is one of the world's fashion superstars. She has come to embody those elements of British creativity – the cultural export of ideas, style, anarchy, history, irony and multi-layers of culture – that have inspired new international directions.

There is an exploratory edge to Westwood's work, a risk element that has influenced clothes from the most expensive of couture to the high street. Her genius includes a new approach to the cut of clothes and the impact of her influential ideas such as underwear as outerwear, tights under jackets, the "mini-crini" skirt and the boned corset using eighteenth-century baroque prints. For Westwood, fashion is a way of reappraising history: she embodies the idea that the British creative tradition is literary rather than visual. Indeed Westwood's starting points are words not pictures. Her clothes are quintessentially British and more than any individual, she has helped place London as the world's centre for leading-edge fashion.

Canon Ixus

DATE: 1996
DESIGNER: Canon Design Centre
MANUFACTURER: Canon Cameras, Tokyo, Japan

The Canon Ixus was instantly hailed as a classic of design when it was launched in 1996. One of the smallest cameras on the market, the Ixus is the size of a packet of playing cards: it is only 9 centimetres (3½ inches) wide and six centimetres (2½ inches) high. Much of its appeal comes from the sleek, compact design of the metallic body. However, it is not just its appearance that places the Ixus at the forefront of design, it also represents the latest advance in camera technology, as it is loaded with the Advanced Photo System. This is a new type of film that requires no negatives and allows the user to select any of three different formats when shooting or printing images.

ADATE: 1996
DESIGNER: Apple
Design Team and
Jonathon Ive
MATERIAL: plastic
MANUFACTURER: Apple
Computers, Cupertino,
California, USA

Apple iMac

In 1999, Apple took the world of product design
by storm with the iMac, which is now generally
recognized to be one of the most important
products at the end of the twentieth century.
It has redefined the way computers are perceived,
coming in a range of fashionable colours and
using a sexy aesthetic far removed from previous
computer styling. The design team is headed
by Jonathan Ives, a British designer based in
California. Ives is also a vice-president of the
corporation, reinforcing the importance of the
place of design within the company. Ives' objective
was to create a computer that was fun and easy
to use. It fits neatly into both the home and office
environment. A detailed approach to every aspect
of the product, from materials to the marketing,
had made the iMac a turning point in acessible
design and technology.

Treforchette
Table Lamp

DATE: 1997
DESIGNER: Michele de
Lucchi (born 1951)
MATERIAL: PVC shade
and table forks
MANUFACTURER:
Produzione
Privata, Italy

Produzione Privata is an
experimental range that
produces objects from the
combination and assembly
of simple, pre-existing
components. It comes from
the studio of one of Italy's
best-known designers,
Michele de Lucchi. In the
1980s, de Lucchi established
himself as a designer of
international importance,
producing experimental but
essentially one-off pieces
as well as working as an
industrial designer for a
series of high-profile Italian
companies. Produzione
Privata is a return to small-
scale experiments, which
reflect de Lucchi's interest
in the twentieth-century
idea of the found object.
In his design for Treforchette,
Michele de Lucchi is searching
for a new direction that
assembles ordinary objects
in an unexpected way. He
has used a simple circle of
PVC for the shade, which is
supported by two "ready
made" metal cutlery forks.

109

DATE: 1997
DESIGNER: Karim Rashid (born 1960)
MATERIAL: injection-moulded virgin polypropylene
MANUFACTURER: Umbra

Garbo Waste Bin

Karim Rashid is a young designer based in New York whose packaging for Issey Miyake's perfumes has attracted much acclaim. The Garbo waste bin is typical of Rashid's ability to bring a contemporary feel to a simple utilitarian object. The multi-purpose waste basket is beautiful, elegant, easy to use, suits a multitude of different interior environments such as homes, offices and restaurants but is low priced.

Rashid used polypropylene to make the waste bin, an inexpensive material that is recyclable and available in a variety of colours and finishes. The walls of the bin are thin so that they use as little plastic as possible. The design of the handles allows for great ease of use and the rounded, soft bottom is easy to clean. The bins are designed so that they can be stacked tightly together, which is efficient for shipping purposes and ideal for creating highly visible and beautiful displays in stores.

Eden

COMPLETION: 2000
St Austell, Cornwall,
England
ARCHITECT: Nicholas
Grimshaw and
Partners, London,
England

A phenomenon since it was
opened officially in April 2001
– with nearly 2 million vistors
by the end of that year – the
Eden project comprises two
huge biospheres situated in
an abandoned quarry in
southwest England. With
funding from the UK
Millennium Commission,
the Eden project was a
collaboration between a team
of highly acclaimed architects,
engineers, surveyors and
project managers aiming to
create an environmental
centre for the new
millennium.

Each of the biospheres
re-creates a different aspects
of the Earth's environment
from the rainforest to the
temperate regions. The
structures are built to adapt to
their particular climate; the
framework is light and flexible
so that it can be shifted and
changed as necessary.

Picture Credits